LIZ FIELDING'S

LITTLE BOOK
of
WRITING
ROMANCE

Classic
Romance

Interior format by The Killion Group
http://thekilliongroupinc.com

Cover design by N J Allsopp

This book is dedicated to all the wonderful editors who have eased the path through my own personal writing journey with special thanks to Gillian Green, Ceri Davies, Emma Dunford and Bryony Green.

Thank you all for your encouragement, your patience and the Champagne.

Thanks too, to Donna Alward for her help and suggestions.

It is also dedicated to the Romantic Novelists' Association and the dozens of fabulous romance authors from all over the world I've met and corresponded with during the last twenty years.
Thanks for the friendship, the fun, for just being there.

Finally, but most important of all, it is dedicated with all my heart to my endlessly supportive husband and children, who ignored the dust, ate the takeaways and cheered me every step of the way

TABLE OF CONTENTS

The first rule of writing is that there are no rules.

WRITING ROMANCE

THIS little book is a primer, an entry level aid for the writer who has a story to tell, but is struggling to get it out of her head and onto paper. To quote the theme song for the movie of Erich Segal's bestselling book Love Story, "How do you begin…"

I know how that feels, I've been there and I have written the book I wish I'd had when I was starting out.

My purpose is to explain, in the simplest terms — no jargon! — and using examples from my own work, how to make the transition from the story in your head to words on paper. How to write a compelling opening, deepen conflict, write honest emotion, hopefully with a touch of humour to leaven the mix. How to write crisp dialogue, develop the romance, add a little sizzle.

It will be useful to anyone who wants to write popular fiction but, before we get down to the nitty-gritty, I'd like to say a few words about romantic fiction in particular. Why readers love it and come back for more.

The primary purpose of a romance novel is to elicit a positive emotional experience for the reader. Make her smile, make her cry, make her sigh with pleasure. To put it in a nutshell, give her a good time.

To achieve that, you must give her characters she will root for, characters who are pursuing a heartfelt passion, a compelling goal, something that really matters.

It might be her career that is driving your heroine, or the protection of her family, or something as basic as survival, but it will be a goal that the reader understands, that she will empathise with, that she will care about.

You must give her characters with whom she's happy to share

hours of her precious time, characters who, no matter what their faults may be — and perfection is so *dull* — are likeable.

Give your reader a hero and heroine who had a life before your book begins, who are meant to be together — who don't just fall in love because you put them together in a book — and who your reader can imagine having a life after the last line.

Real people, taking the journey of their lives.

CHAPTER ONE

GRAB THE READER ON THE FIRST PAGE

Begin your story at a moment of crisis, a point in time when your character's life is about to change for ever.
— Mollie Blake's Writing Workshop Notes from Secret Wedding by Liz Fielding

THE first page of your book makes a promise to the reader. Come with me and I will entertain you, amuse you, warm you, bring a tear to your eye, a sigh of contentment to your heart.

You make that promise by—

- Showing the reader your characters
- Raising questions
- Using dialogue, action, movement to engage the reader's attention

The opening paragraph of any book is a make-or-break moment. It is the moment when you have to convince the reader to buy your book. Not the reader in the bookstore, but the very first and most important reader — the acquiring editor at the publishing house where your manuscript will be just one among the thousands sent to them every year.

It won't have a glossy cover or teasing blurb written by a marketing department, skilled in selling fantasy, to tempt her. It will be a simple, unadorned manuscript, exactly like dozens of others that she will read every week and all you have to grab her attention are your words.

You will have two pages, or maybe three if she's feeling generous, to convince her that your book is worth more than a minute or two of her time.

A great opening to chapter four with a crisis of heart-rending proportions won't help you make a sale if she doesn't get that far.

- The opening is important. Start at the moment of change, the crisis, the day when the clock strikes thirteen.

More, the opening must raise expectations in the reader, set the mood, the style of the book. Ask yourself —

- Is it sharp and direct?
- Is there a mystery to hook her, draw her in?
- Will it tug at the reader's heartstrings?

IS IT SHARP AND DIRECT?

'Fired? What do you mean, you've been fired?'
'Sacked, dismissed, given the heave-ho. Released to explore alternative employment opportunities.'
Again. — The Ordinary Princess

This is a life changing moment. Straight to the point. But it's that "*again*" that draws you in. Who is this? Why can't she hold down a job? What will she do next?

IS THERE A MYSTERY?

When Claudia Beaumont, late and pushing her new sports car hard through the narrow Berkshire lanes, finally spotted the entrance to the airfield, she experienced two distinct and warring emotions. Relief and dread. And dread was winning by a country mile. — Wild Lady

Here the opening suggests that something bad is about to happen. The danger may be unseen but the potential victim is right there, on the page, focussing the reader's attention, attracting her concern. Whatever happens is going to happen to Claudia.

WILL IT WRENCH THE READER'S HEARTSTRINGS?

Funerals and weddings, Sebastian Wolseley hated them both. At least the first had absolved him from attending the more tedious part of the second. And gave him a cast-iron excuse to leave the celebrations once he'd done his duty by one of his oldest friends.

The last thing he felt like doing was celebrating. — The Marriage Miracle

Sebastian Wolseley is having a bad day. A funeral, well that's understandable, but he hates weddings, too. Okay, he's a bloke and weddings are not their thing, but "hate" is a very strong word. Why does he feel such antipathy?

'You look as if you could do with something stronger.'

He turned from the depressed contemplation of the glass in his hand to acknowledge the woman who'd broken into his thoughts. She was the sole occupant of a table littered with the remains of the lavish buffet. The only one who had not decamped to the marquee and the dance floor. From the cool, steady way she was looking at him he had the unsettling notion that she'd been watching him, unnoticed, for some time. But then she wasn't the kind of woman you'd notice.

'Do you tap dance for an encore?' he asked.

She lifted her eyebrows, but she didn't smile. 'Tap dance?'

'You're not the cabaret? A mind-reading act, perhaps?' He heard the biting sarcasm coming from his mouth and wished he'd walked. He had no business inflicting his black mood on innocent bystanders. Or sitters.

The conversation begins and dialogue gives the writer the opportunity to let the reader glimpse the dark world Sebastian Wolseley is inhabiting at that moment. When his companion suggests that he'd be more at home at a wake than a wedding reception, he replies —

'...I have the feeling that the wake I've just left will by now be making this party look sedate.'

And then he felt really guilty.

First he'd been rude to the woman, and when that hadn't driven her away he'd tried to embarrass her. Apparently without success. She merely tilted her head slightly to the side, reminding him of an inquisitive bird.

'Was it someone close?' she enquired, rejecting the usual hushed, reverential tones more usually adopted when speaking to the recently bereaved. She might just as easily have been asking if he'd like a cup of tea.

Such matter-of-factness was an oddly welcome respite from the madness that had overtaken his life in the last week and for the first time in days he felt a little of the tension slip away.

The opening gives us Sebastian Wolseley and the heroine on the page from the first line. It raises questions. Who died, and why the "riotous" wake? What madness has overtaken Sebastian's life? Who is this woman you wouldn't notice, but who he *is* noticing, and why is she alone at a wedding when everyone else is in the marquee dancing?

We see the connection made. He is not attracted by her appearance but by her character. He is drawn in and so, hopefully, is the reader.

- The opening tells the reader who the story is about.
- The opening asks questions.
- The opening intrigues the reader and pulls her into the lives of these two people.

Keep the opening focussed on the main characters. Don't confuse the reader by introducing competition for the hero or heroine at this point; any other characters in the opening scenes should be clearly defined as supporting actors. Not two-dimensional, but secondary.

You don't need back story at this point. You don't need to describe the setting. You don't need to describe the character's physical appearance. If you intrigue her, amuse her, raise her pulse a little, your reader will follow you and will happily wait until you're ready to flesh out the details.

Think of your book as if it were a play or a film.

The curtain rises, the camera rolls—

Action!

You don't believe me?

Go to the library — it's the writer's personal university and it's free. Take down a stack of recently published bestselling books in your chosen genre and read the opening paragraphs. Put aside the ones that grab you. Take them home and study them.

What was it about those few words made you want to read on?

Re-read those opening paragraphs and write down everything you learn.

It won't be what the weather is doing, unless the weather is the inciting incident, the force for change that drives the story. It won't be where the heroine was born, or went to school, or what she's been doing with her life for the past twenty odd years,

Does the writer hold off with the story until the reader is certain we know the identity of our hero or heroine? Where the book is set? What brought them to this point in their lives?

No.

She begins with the moment when her heroine's world is about to change.

Here are some great first lines to be going on with: —

"One hot August Thursday afternoon, Maddie Farraday reached under the front seat of her husband's Cadillac and pulled out a pair of black lace underpants. They weren't hers." —Tell Me Lies, Jennifer Crusie

Tammy was up a tree when royalty arrived. —Her Royal Baby by Marion Lennox

The last of Rachel Stone's luck ran out in front of the Pride of Carolina Drive-In. — Dream a Little Dream, Susan Elizabeth Phillips

These opening lines tell you who the story is about. They intrigue. They draw you in.

You want to know what Maddie Farraday will do next. Why royalty has come calling, unexpectedly, on Tammy. What is about to happen to Rachel Stone at the Pride of Carolina Drive-In.

Learn from the authors of your favourite books, the kind of books you want to write.

START WITH SOMETHING HAPPENING

For the romance writer there are certain major life-changing events which offer great curtain-raisers. Death, birth, coming of age, marriage, starting a new job, losing a job, are all turning points.

The beginning of a book is a moment of change, the unexpected. Consider the wedding. The expected is that the bride and groom will say 'I do' and live happily ever after. The unexpected is —

- when vicar asks if anyone knows just cause or impediment why the wedding cannot take place and someone bursts into the church and says, "Stop! That woman is my wife!"
- when the groom turns to the bride and says 'Smile sweetheart ... this is supposed to be the happiest day of your life.'
- when the vicar asks the bride if she will take this man to be her lawfully wedded husband and her response is to pick up her skirts, dash back down the aisle and leap onto a passing bus.

There is clearly a crisis that has brought the heroine to this point but, given sufficient incentive to read on, the reader will enjoy the fall out and be content to wait for the details.

Consider any newspaper story. It doesn't start with ten years of back story, it starts with a headline.

- LONG LOST HUSBAND HALTS WEDDING
- GIRL WEDS TO SAVE FATHER FROM BANKRUPTCY
- BRIDE DESERTS GROOM AT ALTAR

They are designed to catch your attention, make you read on.
Does your story start with a headline?

- A romance novel starts with a moment of crisis, of change.
- Write the newspaper headline for your story and start from that point.

GET THE HERO AND HEROINE ON THE PAGE

In each of those headline wedding scenarios the heroine is front and centre of the action, the star of her own story. Her co-star, with equal billing, is the hero.

These are the most important characters in a romance. The sooner you can introduce them the better.

- On the first page is good.
- In the first paragraph is better.
- In the first line if at all possible.

'Lukas?' Georgette Bainbridge felt her mouth go dry at her father's suggestion. 'You want me to work for Lukas?' The day which had begun so badly suddenly became a disaster. — An Image of You

Lukas, the hero, does not appear in person until the end of the first chapter. But his presence is there from the opening line of the book, driving every decision the heroine makes and the reader will recognise his status instantly.

'Got you, Chay Buchanan!' Sophie Nash's triumphant exclamation was a tightly contained whisper. — Prisoner of the Heart

Chay Buchanan is being watched through the viewfinder of a camera. The reader is there, looking through it, along with the heroine. Seeing what she's seeing, feeling the same emotional turmoil. There is no doubt whose story this is.

The reader is like a newly hatched chick, programmed to bond with the first likely character she meets.

Make sure that it's your hero or heroine.

- *Cassandra Cornwell had a problem ...*
- *Tom Brodie regarded the man sitting behind the ornate desk ...*
- *'Miss Carpenter?' The enquiry was simply a formality ...*

Keep the action moving during that important first scene. Having grabbed her attention, don't let it wander. Novice writers tend to use too much description. Characters come alive on the page through their actions, not through a detailed inventory of their looks, or their clothes. A detail, an impression that tells you as much about character as looks, is more effective than an itemised list of features.

...as she walked towards him a sudden shaft of sunlight lit up the raindrops that clung to her.
They sparkled against the silver-grey velvet cloak that swirled around her ankles. Sparkled in the spray of flowers she was carrying. Sparkled on long dark lashes that curtained her eyes. —
The Bachelor's Baby

- Description slows down the action

In those first few paragraphs, you want movement, pace, great dialogue. This is the first page of one of my early Mills & Boon romances, *A POINT OF PRIDE.*

'Smile, sweetheart ... this is supposed to be the happiest day of your life.'

What is the most important word in that line? '*... supposed ...*'

Not by one flicker of her lashes did Casey O'Connor acknowledge that she had heard the words murmured by the tall grey-clad figure of Gil Blake as he took her right hand firmly in his own.
She stared resolutely ahead, her face almost the colour of her exquisitely simple ivory silk dress. The vicar smiled reassuringly and then turned to Gil. The wedding service moved inexorably on.

He's wearing a morning coat, she's in ivory silk. Those few words inform the reader that this is not some ramshackle, hole-in-wall wedding. It is a full-dress occasion. A major social event.

He takes her hand firmly in his. He is in control. '*The wedding service moved inexorably on.*' The words are doom laden, reinforcing the conviction that this wedding is not the normal happy-ever-event.

Happy people do not make for exciting reading.

'I Gilliam Edward Blake take thee Catherine Mary O'Connor ...'
Gil's firm voice rang firmly through the church, every word clearly
heard by the congregation come to witness the shockingly sudden
marriage of Casey O'Connor to the tall, tanned stranger who had
snatched her from under the very nose of the most eligible bachelor
in Melchester.'

- Shockingly sudden
- Stranger
- Snatched

Those words hammer home the message. But there is a lot more
information in that paragraph. Casey may not be happy, but Gil
Blake's *'firm voice'* tells the reader that he is well satisfied with
events.

Tall, tanned stranger.

Where has he come from? The tan suggests somewhere warm.
And he's snatched her from *'... under the very nose of the most*
eligible bachelor in Melchester.' What hold does he have over her
that would make her desert such a man and agree to a marriage that
she clearly does not want?

The minister, satisfied with the groom's response, turned to her.
"I Catherine Mary O'Connor take thee Gilliam ...' he prompted.

As she heard the words that would bind them together the
temptation to flee was so strong that she was uncertain whether she
had in fact stepped back, or if it was just her imagination that Gil's
fingers tightened possessively over hers.

She glanced nervously at him from under her lashes. His grey
eyes regarded her steadily, but there was no warmth to encourage
her response. He was demanding her total surrender.'

The way characters are feeling is more important than what they
are wearing. He is in control and knows it. She is unhappy and that
raises a question. He knows she's unhappy and he doesn't appear to
care. That makes it a story.

One page in and the reader knows a lot about these characters, the
least important of which is the colour of Gil Blake's eyes.

Have another look at those books you brought home from the

library and see how much solid information the writer has crammed into the first page. How much she has told you about the characters, about what is happening to them, drawing you into the book so that you want to read on?

GRAB THE READER'S ATTENTION

- Show the reader the characters
- Use action
- Introduce conflict

Consider how they do it in the movies. First they show you the character, walking down the street in her neighbourhood, maybe.

- 'Hi, Grace! How're the wedding plans coming along?' Grace Darling smiled at her neighbour...

Or working in her office.

- 'Grace? You coming for lunch?' Grace Darling grabbed her jacket...

Perhaps having dinner in a restaurant with her husband, celebrating their first wedding anniversary.

- 'John, I'm so happy.' Grace Darling reached for her husband's hand...

Then they introduce action.

- Grace, still laughing and talking with her neighbour, steps off the kerb and is mown down by a speeding car.
- The phone in the office rings. Grace hesitates and then goes back to answer it.
- In the restaurant Grace looks up as a woman approaches the table.

A story has begun.
What happens next is the point on which the story turns.

- The man sitting beside Grace's hospital bed tells her that she has a serious spinal injury.
- Grace answers the phone and is told by the caller that he has taken her child.
- The woman produces a gun and shoots Grace's husband.

Whatever happens next, Grace's life has been tossed into the maelstrom of her story and her life has changed forever.

The beginning is written.
The reader is hooked.

TO SUM UP

- Begin with the moment of change
- Show the reader your characters
- Use action and dialogue
- Introduce conflict
- Keep description to a minimum
- Keep explanations for later

CHAPTER TWO

CREATE CHARACTERS YOUR READER WILL CARE ABOUT

A hero has to be strong, tender, a man who would never let down the woman he loves. But he has to be flawed. If he were perfect there would be no story.
— Mollie Blake's Writing Workshop Notes from Secret Wedding by Liz Fielding

ROMANTIC fiction is character led.

A plot, a story is important, but unlike a thriller, where the hero or heroine responds to outside events, romance is driven by emotion, feelings, internal fears and longings and it is the character of your hero and heroine that will dictate how the plot of a romance develops.

Consider the great characters in literature, characters in the books you love. What made them memorable? What made you care about them?

They won't have been perfect; no one wants to read about someone who is perfect, but they will have been determined, wilful, well motivated. Excellent examples include Jane Austen's Emma, Scarlet O'Hara in Gone With the Wind and Vanity Fair's Becky Sharpe.

Readers are looking for a heroine they can identify with, connect with, even if she sometimes gets things wrong.

Imagine you were in a lift, stuck between floors, and there was only one other occupant. Would you want to be confined with a moaning man, a whining woman, someone of either sex having hysterics? Or would be want to be with someone calm and practical, someone who would amuse you, who would make the time pass quickly?

Ask yourself if your hero and heroine have the "lift factor".

WHO IS YOUR HEROINE?

- Is she sympathetic, likeable, fun? Is she real? We all have flaws — your heroine should not be perfect! Why would a reader care about her?
- What does she long for? What is her driving passion? What choices would she make under pressure? Does she want to be the boss or is she content to be the secretary?
- What is she afraid of? What emotional armour is she wearing?
- Who, what — if she found the courage of break free of the protective front she wears — does she have the potential to become?
- Would your reader want to spend precious hours in her company? Would she want her as her best friend?

WHO IS YOUR HERO?

- What demon is driving him?
- Is his motivation clear and believable?
- What are his most admirable qualities, his strengths?
- What is his weakness? What emotional scars does he carry?
- Who, or what, would he die for?
- Will your reader fall in love with him?

Your reader is going to be with these characters for several hours of her precious time, but forget her for a moment; as a writer you're going to be living with them in your head for weeks, months. Make sure they are people you want to spend time with.

Always ask yourself, what they could do that is more ingenious, dramatic, surprising or funny.

HERE ARE SOME MORE QUESTIONS ABOUT YOUR CHARACTER

EXTERNAL

What does he or she fear physically?
- Heights, the dark, open spaces
- Spiders, mice, cockroaches
- Water
- Dogs, cats, horses
- Speed, lifts, escalators
- Injections, pain
- What do you fear?

Ask yourself what happened to trigger that fear.
Confront your character with his or her worst nightmare.
How will they react? Who will they turn to for help?

INTERNAL

What does your character fear emotionally?

- Loss of status
- Poverty
- Betrayal
- Rejection
- Loneliness
- Risk
- Failure
- Loss of something vital to his or her family – home, land, business
- What do you fear?

Ask yourself what happened to trigger that fear.
Confront them with the worst that can happen.
How will they react? Who will they turn to for help?

GETTING TO KNOW THEM

To write their story you will have to know your characters

intimately. For this, you need to do more than fill out a character worksheet with all their physical characteristics, their birth sign, their place in the family hierarchy, the names of their siblings.

Of course you have to know what colour eyes and hair your hero has, how tall he is, how old he is — ditto your heroine — before you begin. Making a note of these details and pinning it up so that you can check them when you're in full flow a hundred pages into your manuscript is a sensible precaution. (You may think you couldn't possibly forget these vital statistics but you will.)

These are, however, no more than the basics.

To come alive on the page, your hero and heroine must be more than two-dimensional cardboard cut-outs that you move around the stage. You should not be asking yourself "what can I make them do next". If your characters are blood-and-bones, heart-and-soul real, you will know what they would do, just as you instinctively know what someone close to you would do in any given circumstance.

You may hear authors talking about characters who "take over" the story. That is not because the author is not in control of her characters, but because she has created three-dimensional, living, breathing people, men and women she knows so well that her writing brain is flying ahead of her fingers on the keyboard.

To truly know your characters you must understand not just what they look like, where they went to school, what they do for a living but see them living in their own world, having a life before you write Chapter One.

That world will dictate what you need to create them.

First you will need a name.

You can Google websites to find the most popular names for any year. Make sure you use one for the country in which your character was born. Fashions in names are cyclical and vary quite markedly from country to country.

Think about social class. A name will brand your character, possibly embarrass a character who has moved light years from his or her start in life. How will he or she deal with that?

Think about the image you want to portray.

And think about your reader, too. There are many beautiful names out there, but if you give your heroine an ethnic name that the reader is unfamiliar with, is unsure how to pronounce, she will stumble over it every time she sees it and it will throw her out of the story.

It is, of course, possible to make the fact that no one can spell her name if she says it, or pronounce it if they see it written down, part of her character. When she demonstrates how to pronounce it to the thick hero in tiny little chunks of sound, it will give you a chance to show them both in action, and give the reader a break.

Think, too, about how your hero and heroine speak. If they are Irish, or from the southern states of the United States, or the Caribbean islands, for example, they will have a slightly different rhythm to their speech. Don't make a big thing of it and never write in dialect; it really is hard work to read and popular contemporary fiction should be effortlessly entertaining.

By all means use a native term of endearment, the occasional word to remind the reader that the character has a distinctive voice and cultural background, but if you allow the reader to hear the heroine listening to the hero, or vice versa, the reader will get it.

Low and gravelly, it was the voice of a man you just knew it wouldn't be wise to mess with. Yet his impatience was softened by velvet undertones. Sort of like Sean Connery, but without the Scottish accent. — City Girl in Training

And then there was her voice.
No one spoke like that unless they were born to it. Not even twenty-five thousand pounds a year at Dower House could buy that true-blue aristocratic accent, a fact he knew to his cost. — Christmas Angel for the Billionaire

'Still got a temper then, cariad?' The voice was soft as a shawl of mist around the shoulders of Carreg Cennen. Welsh as the daffodil attached to his lapel for St David. — Dangerous Flirtation

These people, these characters do not step onto the pages of your book fresh-minted. They have families, friends, they will have gone on holiday, had jobs, been moulded by their experiences for many years before you step into their lives at this point of crisis, of change, of opportunity.

To familiarise yourself with their world you need to walk in their shoes.

HAVE YOUR HEROINE—

- wait for a bus. Where is she going? Is she chatting to the people around her? Lost in thought? Is this an unusual experience for her, or could she do it in her sleep?
- walk around a supermarket. Is it budget, a posh food hall, or somewhere in between? Has she bought ready meals? Ready prepared vegetables? No vegetables? What kind of biscuits, coffee, bread did she choose? Has she bought pet food? Champagne? What did she buy that isn't food?
- look for a job. Will she check newspaper ads, register with an online agency, look in the newsagent's window?
- deal with a domestic emergency. A washing machine flood, a stove-top fire, mice. Think of your worst nightmare and confront her with it.
- take exercise. Does she play a round of golf? Go to the gym? Walk to work? Walk to the fridge?
- take care of animals (not necessarily her own.) How would she cope with cleaning out a hamster cage? Giving a cat a pill? Where would she take a dog for a walk?
- work with a colleague she dislikes, cope with a dissatisfied customer, take care of a tired child.
- spend the evening alone.
- look for something to wear for a special occasion. Will she go to a boutique? A department store? High street budget chain? A charity shop? Borrow from a friend?
- drive a car. Parallel park. Get a ticket for speeding.
- have a manicure. Professional, or do-it-yourself? Are her nails neat, or long and painted, or false, or bitten?
- turn on the radio. Which station will she choose?
- choose a book or magazine to read on a train.
- get a tattoo.

Then have your hero do the same.

Okay, maybe not the nail polish.

Very little — maybe none — of this will make it into a book. Like all research you should work on the iceberg principle; no more than an eighth is ever on show. It doesn't matter. Your familiarity with the way they live, deal with challenges, cope with incidents that take them out of their comfort zone will shine through on the page and convince the reader that they had a life before they stepped onto the pages of your book.

CONSISTENCY

Your characters must be consistent in their—

- thoughts
- actions
- fears

If your heroine is afraid of dogs in chapter one, for instance, she can't suddenly lose that fear and be romping with the Great Dane in chapter six without something happening to resolve her problem.

If her radio is permanently set to a music station that plays rock, or pop, there must be a reason why she'd switch to a jazz or classic station.

If she loses her temper, is that her default mode for every small annoyance? Or is it so rare that, when she's finally driven beyond endurance and snaps, everyone will stop what they're doing to watch, open-mouthed?

If your hero is commitment phobic, he can't suddenly become a man who wants a wife and babies half way through the final chapter. The reader has to see him drawn in, fall in love; he may still be in denial, but when he takes the final step to the life that promises so much more, her response must not be an exasperated, 'I don't think so…', but a triumphant 'Yes!'

YOUR HEROINE'S JOURNEY

From the moment you throw a rock in her path on page one, your heroine is on a journey. For her to reach her destination, you will have to know—

- your heroine's deepest desire
- her passion
- her life's goal

It is not to fall in love and get married.

In *The Bridesmaid's Reward*, Brad Morgan, Dodie Layton's new personal trainer, is listening to her explain why she has to be two dress sizes smaller when she's bridesmaid at her glamorous sister's celebrity wedding.

'How badly do you want this?'
'How badly?'
'I can see the appeal of slimming down for the big occasion—' *although the attraction of dressing up in impractical and outdated clothes simply to witness two people make fools of themselves seemed to have passed him by '—but I'd be happier if you were taking a long-term approach to fitness.'*
'Look, I've discussed this with Gina. Your boss?' she reminded him.
'My boss?'
'I've had the pep talk, okay?'
He swallowed a smile.
'Okay,' he said, 'I just didn't want you making yourself thoroughly miserable in an effort to fit a smaller dress size. Just for one day.'
'Just?' She leaned forward so that her cleavage was once again an unconscious invitation that any man would be delighted to accept. 'Let me tell you this isn't just any old day. I may not be the bride, but if I explain that the best man is going to be Charles Gray, would that clarify the importance of a smaller dress size?'
'Charles Gray?' he queried, distracted.
'You're kidding, right?'
He dragged his gaze back to her face. 'Sorry.'
'Actor?' she offered. 'Movie star? Dark brown eyes that crinkle dangerously at the corner whenever he smiles, floppy corn-coloured hair and seriously cute bottom—'

Is your heroine's motivation clear and believable?

- What will stop her from achieving her goal?

'...Dodie's a comfort eater — big time — and I suspect, for all her excitement, she'll find the stress of being her sister's bridesmaid hard to cope with.'

'You mean she'll be in the nearest pizza parlour the minute I'm out of sight?'

'She won't be able to help herself. She'll need watching.'

'I've noticed. So far she's lied about her weight, her height and her age.'

Will a reader identify with your heroine?

- What is her pain? The unhealed wound that prevents her from being her true self.

''My mother had plans to launch a new theatrical dynasty upon the world. Sadly, I was just not star material. My mother tried, poor woman. I did the classes, but I was a big disappointment. Two-left feet, tone deaf and totally tongue-tied whenever I was asked to perform in public.' She pulled a face. 'Which I suppose, in retrospect, is just as well.'

'You seem to have lost the shyness.'

She gave him a quick look.

'You teach ... taught.'

'That's easy. I know about that stuff. But ask me to recite a poem to a room full of people...' She shuddered at the memory of it. 'It was a huge relief when Natasha joined the baby dance class and proved a natural. I was able to drop out, retire quietly to the corner with a box of coloured pencils and a packet of crisps...'

Will a reader empathise with her?

- What is her fear? What will she have to face to break free? Here she faces the man who betrayed her and wrecked her life. He's about to betray her again.

She'd been aware of the large brown envelope that lay on the table between them. Now he picked it up and handed it to her.

'What is it?' she asked. 'A personal note from the Vice Chancellor?'

'It's a little incentive to be a good girl, Dodie.'

'I resigned as your doormat a year ago,' she said, but without any hint of bitterness — he didn't matter enough for bitterness — as she lifted the flap. Inside was a photograph. The one Brad had taken of her, red-faced, out of breath and looking as if she was about to expire.

'Have you any idea how much the tabloids would pay for a picture of Natasha's big sister getting in shape for the wedding?' he asked.

Do you show her winning through, achieving her true goal?

Dodie's immediate, external need is to look good at her sister's wedding. The gorgeous actor is certainly an incentive to slim down — as chief bridesmaid, she'll get to dance with him, be pictured with him in *Celebrity* magazine. And that's all she's going to tell Brad Morgan. But her real goal is to make her cheating, ambitious, ex see what he's missing. Not her, but an opportunity to network with the rich and famous.

Losing weight, is her outer journey, but she has a bigger battle than beating the bulge. It's not what she looks like on the outside that is crippling her emotionally.

All her life she has been treated by her mother as invisible, a shadow in the star-shine of her glamorous sister. That her cheating ex is more interested in her usefulness to him as a cook, housekeeper — he's demonstrated that he can and does get sex anywhere — and conduit to her famous, well-connected sister only reinforces that lesson.

Her worth as a person in her own right, as a talented artist, has never been acknowledged by anyone who matters to her.

Her internal journey is about self-discovery.

It seems a very simple thing, but most of us will recognise those internal doubts, empathise with her lack of self-worth. All of us will cheer Dodie on as she stands tall, looks her ex in the eye when he attempts to blackmail her into taking him to the wedding as her "plus one" using the hideous "here be dragons" picture — a reminder of her goal — that he'd stolen from her fridge door and tells him to publish and be damned.

YOUR HERO'S JOURNEY

Like your heroine, your hero will go on a journey which, during the course of the book, will change him.

Ask yourself —

- What haunts him?
- Torments him?
- Who are his ghosts?

Jake Hallam, in *The Bachelor's Baby*, is a man incapable of commitment. His high-flying parents wanted a well-behaved child they could take out of the box when occasion demanded. Attention seeking behaviour only caused further distance. First to boarding school and then, finally, into the care system. Complete rejection.

How can you love when you have never been loved? How can you be a father when you've no example to follow?

When Jake meets Amy Jones at a social event in the home of a mutual friend, the sexual attraction is immediate, compelling, irresistible. Mike, their host, who knows them both well and, aware that this will not end well, does his best to prevent the inevitable.

> *'I'll take Amy home,' Jake said.*
> *'You're quite sure? It's out of your way...'*
> *'Quite sure.' He'd been going that way ever since Amy had looked at him. Maybe Mike was right. Maybe she was a witch.*

And when they arrive at her door...

> *...she held out the key to him. It hung there between them, shimmering dull silver in the stormy light and at the back of Jake's mind warning bells began to ring.*
> *'I don't do commitment,' he said roughly. Almost hoping that she would tell him to go. Leave. Get out.*

He knows, on some subliminal level, that this isn't just another brief encounter. Amy presents a very real danger to his avowed avoidance of commitment but, having drawn an emotional line in the sand, he stays. It's just one night he tells her. Tells himself. And the next day he flies across the Atlantic on business. No problem.

Have you made it impossible for your hero to walk away?

- Is he vulnerable? What is his weakness?

At the beginning of the book we see Jake as a successful, strong man who understands his own failings. His no-commitment rule is to protect others rather than himself. There is something about Amy Jones, however, that captivates him, draws him in at first sight. Even with an ocean between them he can't get her out of his mind and he cuts short his trip only to come face to face with his worst nightmare.

What a fool! What an idiot!
What on earth had possessed him? He was a man with "precaution" stamped on his brain. Mike had as good as warned him. Take care, he'd said. He hadn't added, she'll bewitch you.

From the beginning it is clear that the prospect of fatherhood terrifies Jake Hallam. It will be a while before the reader learns the reason, but in the meantime, she enjoys his confusion as Amy tells him, with complete sincerity, that he need not worry, that she understood the no-commitment message and doesn't expect him to be involved.

Standing on the threshold, his thoughts in turmoil, he realised that he didn't want to go. He just didn't know how to stay.

Is he empathetic? Will your reader feel for him?

- What is his strength?

Jake decides that Amy wants a baby with a rich daddy — without the tiresome bother of a husband. When she returns the very large cheque he's sent by courier — his attempt to buy the freedom to forget — he naturally assumes that it isn't as big as she'd hoped and goes to see her. She makes it clear that he is quite wrong, which annoys him, confuses him. He needs closure and she won't give it to him.

Most men would have taken the hint, probably thanked their lucky stars and left it at that. Jacob Hallam wasn't most men. He didn't want to get involved but he couldn't walk away. His conscience wouldn't let him.

He was in for a bad time, she thought. And felt an unexpected twinge of pity for him.

Amy's right. She wants him, more than anything in the world, but she does nothing to hold him, refuses all help and insists that he's free to walk away.

He cannot accept that. He made a mistake and he has to pay for it.

Jake tries everything. Money has failed, so he hires a housekeeper to take care of her. Amy subverts his intention by having her take care of other people in the village. He decorates the nursery himself — having figured out that if he hires a professional she will set him to painting the dilapidated village hall. He even drives her to an antenatal class when he discovers that she's taking the bus. Then he discovers her one weakness and, when she breaks down, he believes he has finally won.

The reader sees him being drawn in chapter by chapter, giving the one thing he swears he is incapable of giving, himself. He doesn't see it that way. He believes he's doing all this so that he can walk away with a clear conscience.

It isn't until he believes her life, their unborn baby's life, is in danger that he is finally brought face to face with reality. Finally understands how far over the line he has stepped.

What will your hero do for your heroine — short of changing his life?

- What will he change in his life, in himself, for the sake of the heroine?

Until he meets Amy, Jake's only commitment is to his business empire. Even when he rushes to her side after the accident he has still not, in his head, taken the final step.

It is only when Amy, no longer able to cope with the situation, tells him that she doesn't want to see him again that he is forced to confront a future without her. At this point he finally chooses the risk of loving her, being a father, over the arid, safe, pain-free life to which he has been clinging, limpet-like, ever since they met.

There had been no mistaking her warning glance when he'd reached out on automatic to gently place his palm over the infant lying safe beneath her breast. It had all the power of a hand-off from a rugby prop forward.

And it had hurt just as much. A warning of how it would feel if he could never return, never touch her, never hold her again. Was that the pain people called love? How could you tell that it was real? That it would last? How could he say the words when he didn't know?

The driver was waiting.

'No. Take me to Maybridge.' He took his cellphone from his overnight bag and called Maggie.

'Jake, for heaven's sake, where are you? I've set up a video conference—'

'Maggie,' he said, cutting her off. 'Do you remember that conversation we had about what would happen if I ever happened to fall under a bus?'

'I was speaking metaphorically.'

'Well, metaphorically, it's just happened.'

Does your hero change, grow, throughout the course of the book?

CHARACTER ARC

The journey from the world in which the character has been living at the opening of the book — behind the safety of the false front constructed for the world to see — to the true self, is known as the character "arc".

There is no magic to it.

Real characters, facing a solid internal conflict will naturally create the arc of growth, setback, growth through the course of your book. Your hero, your heroine, will take two steps forward, one step back. There will be a final, panicked attempt to cling to the familiar before taking the final step to become the person he or she has the potential to be.

When your character accepts that truth, embraces it, the payoff is much more than a satisfying ending; it is the beginning of a new, richer life. At that moment, when your reader can picture your hero and heroine living in the future, becoming a family, you have delivered on your promise of a happy ever after.

TO SUM UP

- Is your heroine likeable, empathetic, spirited? Would you want to spend time with her?
- What is her deepest desire? Is her motivation clear?
- What does she fear — emotionally, physically?
- Who would she die for?

- Will your reader fall in love with your hero? Is he deep-down strong?
- What haunts him?
- What does he fear — emotionally, physically?
- Who would he die for?

- What will each of them need to confront in order to achieve their potential?

CHAPTER THREE

ENSURE YOUR CONFLICT IS BIG ENOUGH TO CARRY THE STORY

Keep the conflict simple. Make sure the reader knows what's going on. Ask yourself...Is this conflict strong enough to sustain the length of the story?
— from Mollie Blake's Writing Workshop Notes from Secret Wedding by Liz Fielding

WHAT IS CONFLICT?

FIRST, most importantly, it is not two characters having an argument for 199 pages and then saying "I love you" on page 200.

While your characters may be fighting one another on page one – arguing, bickering, in direct conflict because of an external situation, the reader has to see them growing throughout the book, in understanding, in attraction. She has to see them falling in love.

She has to see them coming to terms with their inner demons and becoming bigger people as a result. She has to believe in their happy ending; more, to believe they have earned it.

An event that delays a hero or heroine's progress towards a goal is not conflict, it is only an incident.

A misunderstanding, a wrong assumption, one or other of the characters jumping to the wrong conclusion is not conflict. Conflict lies in the underlying reasons why they are unable to communicate.

Meddling by another person is not conflict and can make the main characters appear weak, passive, unable to take charge of their own lives. Nor is the main character's unwillingness to admit that they are attracted to the hero or heroine in any way, conflict. They might fight off the attraction, but conflict lies in the underlying reasons why they fight instead of fall into bed.

So what, in the context of a novel, is conflict?

Imagine the very worst person that your hero or heroine could fall in love with. Then double the nightmare. Tighten the screw. Layer in more reasons why this match is impossible. Family feud, faith, social class, distance, politics, health, reputation, a past relationship, secrets, lies, perceived past betrayal.

Conflict comes when, despite all and every apparently good reason for the characters to say "no way", the attraction is too powerful for them to walk away, as in these partnerships that should never have worked.

- A sheikh and a single-mother with a dark secret.

Diana could not believe this was happening. There were still people about—Zahir's kind of people, men in dinner jackets, women in evening clothes heading towards the fashionable nightclubs in the area to celebrate some special occasion. Laughing, joking, posing as someone took photographs with a camera phone.

Maybe if she'd been dressed in a glamorous gown she wouldn't have felt so foolish. But in her uniform...

'Don't!' she begged, but Zahir caught her hand, and humming, began to spin her along the footpath. 'Zahir...' Then, 'For heaven's sake that's not even the right tune!'

'No? How does it go?'

Maybe his excitement, his joy, were infectious, but somehow, before she knew it, she was singing it to him, filling gaps in the words with da-da-de-dums and he was humming and they were dancing around Berkeley Square to a song that was old when her parents had first danced to it. A song in which the magic of falling in love made the impossible happen. Made London a place where angels dined, where nightingales sang and where the streets were paved with stars. — The Sheikh's Unsuitable Bride

- A playboy banker and a paraplegic artist.

'You like to dance?' she asked.

He had the oddest feeling that he was being tested in some way.
'Yes, but we can pass if you're hungry. Go straight to dinner.'
'And are you good?'
Definitely tested.
'At dancing?'
'That's what we were talking about,' she reminded him.
'Was it?' He didn't think so, but he played along. 'I decline to
answer that question on the grounds that it might incriminate me.'
'Come, come. No false modesty, please.' She lifted her head,
listening to the music coming from the marquee, then shook her
head. 'No, that's a waltz. Everyone can waltz. Can you foxtrot?'
'Hasn't that been banned?' he enquired.
'Too advanced for you, hmm? How about a tango, then?'
'Without treading on your toes? That I couldn't guarantee, but
give me a rose to clutch beneath my teeth and I'm willing to give it a
try.'
Her laugh was wholehearted and her mouth didn't disappoint.
'Well, that's certainly the best offer I've had for quite a while, but
don't panic. Nothing is getting me out of this chair for the rest of the
evening.' — The Marriage Miracle

- A romance fiction-loving cleaner and an academic.

If she'd been the wraithlike heroine of one of those top shelf
romances — or indeed of her own growing pile of unpublished
manuscripts — Ellie would, at this point, have dropped tidily into his
arms and the fool, having taken one look, would have fallen instantly
and madly in love with her. Of course there would have to be several
hundred pages of misunderstandings and confusion before he finally
admitted it either to himself or to her since men tended to be a bit
dense when it came to romance.
Since this was reality, and she was built on rather more
substantial lines than the average heroine of a romance — who
wasn't? — she fell on him like the proverbial ton of bricks and they
went down in a heap of tangled limbs.
And Emily Bronte gave him a cuff round the ear with her leather
binding for good measure.
'Idiot!' she finally managed but, winded by her fall, the word
lacked force. Ellie sucked in some air and tried again. 'Idiot!' —

much better — 'You might have killed me!' Then, because he'd somehow managed to walk through locked doors into a house she was caretaking — as in "taking care of" — she demanded, 'Who the hell are you, anyway?'

Then, as her brain finally caught up with her mouth — and because burglars rarely stopped to exchange must-read titles with their victims — the answer hit her with almost as much force as she'd landed on him.

There was only one person he could be.

Dr Benedict Faulkner.

The Dr Benedict Faulkner whose house she was sitting.

The Dr Benedict Faulkner who was supposed to be on the other side of the world, up to his eyes in ancient tribal split infinitives. — The Secret Life of Lady Gabriella.

Conflict comes when, despite all and every good reason for the characters to go their separate ways, outside influences conspire to keep them together.

- The brittle, emotionally-damaged socialite and the hard-nosed archaeologist trapped underground.

She was half way to her feet when his hand, sweeping the air in the direction of her voice, connected with her leg and grabbed it. She let out a shriek of alarm

'Shut up,' he said, tightly. 'I've got a headache and I can't think with all that noise.'

'Poor baby,' she crooned, with crushing insincerity. Then lashed out with her free leg, her toe connecting with his thigh.

He jerked her other leg from beneath her which was a mistake since she landed on top of him.

He said one word, but since she'd knocked the breath out him, only he knew for certain what it was. — Wedded in a Whirlwind.

- A newly bereaved heroine forced into a paper marriage in order to protect the future of an assortment of dependents.

'This is a joke.' She looked to the lawyer for back up. 'This is Steven's idea of a practical joke...' If she'd hoped they would both

laugh and admit it, she was disappointed. Tom looked down at his desk as if he wished he was anywhere else. Guy continued to look at her, waiting for her answer.

'Let me see.'

He surrendered the folder and its contents to her and she looked at them. Tickets, honeymoon suite, wedding ceremony. But it was Guy's name on the documents, not his own.

'This is unbelievable.'

'It's a formality, Francesca. A paper marriage. Breathing space for you to sort yourself out.'

'I don't need breathing space. I certainly don't need you. I just need somewhere to live.'

'You and Toby, Matty and Connie need somewhere to live,' he corrected. — A Wife on Paper

Conflict is a force for change.

By living through it, the hero and heroine will become different people from those who appeared on page one. They will have faced their fears, walked through the fire and earned their happy ever after.

Even in the most action based novels, if the protagonist doesn't have something personal at stake you may have trouble maintaining reader interest. This is especially important in the case of romance novels.

'Give me a chance, Sadie. I won't let you down.'

Sadie touched her shoulder, a gesture that said she understood. 'Let's see how it goes today shall we?'

Okay. She got the message. This was her opportunity to show what she could do; it was up to her to make the most of it. — The Sheikh's Unsuitable Bride

There are two basic types of conflict: internal and external.

It is possible to write and sell books that lean heavily to one side or the other but a combination of the two works best.

Both types of conflict should be ongoing, active and changing as the story progresses.

External conflict is basically one that someone or something else can resolve. With the external conflict the reader will be able to see ways out of the problem.

Internal conflict is a war that takes place within a person. It is the part of character that fights commitment; it forms blockages to relationships, retreats from any situation that involves taking a risk, a step in the dark. It is, at its most basic, fear of pain, fear of rejection, fear of failure.

These emotional barriers are shaped by a character's personal history and your characters would rather walk through fire than confront them. These are the conflicts that they will have to do battle with, and conquer, during the course of the story.

On a higher plain it will involve protecting not just self, but someone or something else.

In *The Bride's Baby*, a simple conversation between the hero and heroine would have cleared up all misunderstandings, but it was the reason neither of them could have that conversation that was the underlying internal conflict.

He didn't move, but continued to regard her with those relentlessly fierce eyes that were apparently hell-bent on scrambling her brains.

The man she dreaded seeing. The man she longed more than anything to see, talk to. If he would just give her a chance, let her show him a scan of the baby they'd made. His daughter. But maybe he understood the risk, the danger of being sucked into a relationship he'd never asked for, never wanted.

She'd given him that get-out-of-jail free card and could not take it back. And since he was studiously avoiding the subject, clearly he had no intention of voluntarily surrendering it.

They had both been jilted days before their weddings and had built up years of the armour plating that I talked about in the chapter on character. On the surface they are both strong, successful people but, deep down, beneath the front they show to the world, is the fear of rejection.

In Sylvie's case — jilted when her family lost everything — it is the fear that she is not worthy of someone's wholehearted till-death-us-do-part love without the financial backing of a wealthy and influential family.

Tom, who has come from nothing and yearns for acceptance, social status to match his billions, has been jilted by his high-society bride; dumped for a poverty-stricken aristocrat. The coronet trumping the billions.

The fact that Sylvie comes from the same aristocratic background to his runaway bride only heightens his internal conflict. He's been badly — and publicly — burned and isn't about to play with fire again.

A simple conversation would clear up all misunderstandings. Talking, however, is the one thing they cannot do because to say the words would lay each of them open to that which they most fear. Rejection.

Internal conflict adds meaning and complexity to a story, arising as it does from problems tied up so closely with who they are.

The child from a broken home will have a different view of marriage to one coming from a settled background, for instance.

It was Tolstoy who said that all happy families resemble one another, but each unhappy family is unhappy in its own way. Unhappy families are fertile breeding grounds for internal conflict in your characters.

Fear of betrayal, abandonment, poverty. These mould our characters, form blockages to their relationships. Belle, in *Reunited: Marriage in a Million*, fears poverty above all things.

'I was fourteen. An angry teenager who'd lived rough for the best part of three years, on the run from my mother's demons, from social services. Scavenging to live, seeing things that no child...'

Elle, in *Tempted By Trouble,* fears anything that threatens the fragile stability of the family that she's holding together by sheer willpower and hard work.

She also fears her sexuality. Her mother was a flighty piece who believed in free love and had three daughters to prove it – but no father to support any of them. Her grandmother had lost all their money to a conman who flattered to deceive.

The arrival of a vintage ice cream van, delivered by a man who sparks her suppressed sexuality into flaming life is the inciting incident that starts the story, bringing both internal and an external conflict into the forefront of our heroine's life.

Internal, because Sean is her worst nightmare come true. The irresistible man.

Elle had begun to believe that she'd bypassed the genetic tick that reduced all Amery women to putty in the presence of a good looking man.

Caught off guard, she discovered that she'd been fooling herself.

The only reason she'd escaped so far, it seemed, was because until this moment she hadn't met a man with eyes of that particularly intense shade of blue.

A man with shoulders wide enough to carry the troubles of the world and tall enough not to make her feel awkward about her height, which had been giving her a hard time since she'd hit a growth spurt somewhere around her twelfth birthday. With a voice that seemed to whisper right through her bones until it reached her toes.

Even now they were curling inside her old trainers in pure ecstasy.

He epitomised the casual, devil-may-care, bad-boy look of the travelling men who, for centuries, had arrived on the village common in the first week of June with the annual fair and departed a few days later, leaving a trail of broken hearts and the occasional fatherless baby in their wake.

Trouble.

External because she already has more than enough trouble. She doesn't want anything to do with the van and tries all ways to get out of taking on a load of trouble. The two are inextricably linked because, when she accepts that she has no choice but to take on the burden of the van, she has to accept Sean's help.

'Time to drum up some custom.'

'Does that mean I get to play the jingle?'

'You'll have to learn how, first.'

'Okay,' she said, looking over the dashboard. 'What do I push?'

'Push?'

'I assumed there'd be a button or something. To start the disk?'

'Disk? Please! This is a vintage vehicle, madam. Built before the age of seatbelts and the internet.'

'Oh, right. The dark ages. So, what do you do?'

'This,' he said, taking hold of a handle beside him in the driver's

door. 'You wind it up here, then switch it on and off here.' He demonstrated and a ripple of Greensleeves filled the air. 'Your turn.'

Elle regarded the far door. To reach the chime she'd have to lean right across Sean. Get dangerously close to those firm thighs and what was undoubtedly a six-pack beneath the soft linen shirt he was wearing.

'I can't reach,' she said.

He leaned back in his seat. 'How's that?'

'It would be far too dangerous while we're moving,' she said. Miss Sensible.

His response was to slow down, pull over. 'We're not moving now.' — *Tempted by Trouble.*

She grows in courage throughout the book. Learns to trust her sisters, learns to trust Sean, but most of all she learns to trust herself. During the course of the story, both she and Sean take a personal journey and learn important lessons from each other. Even if their romance had been short-lived, died a natural death, they would both, at the end of the story, still have been winners because they had become the people they had the potential to be.

TO SUM UP

- Conflict is a force for change
- Internal conflict is a war that takes place within a person
- External conflict can be resolved without change
- Internal conflict forces a character to confront their fears
- Fully resolved internal conflict will transform your character into the person he or she has the potential to become

CHAPTER FOUR

DIG DEEP FOR EMOTION

The romance reader is looking for warmly observed characters and deeply felt emotion.
— from Mollie Blake's Writing Workshop Notes from Secret Wedding by Liz Fielding

THE writer of romantic fiction is in the emotion business and you will need to tap into your own feelings to get this right. It is the honesty, the reality that you bring to your writing, that will touch your reader, heighten the moment.

We go to extraordinary lengths to find fresh and exciting plots for our stories. I have conjured up desperate boardroom takeover battles, paper marriages, an earthquake – conflict situations that throw our hero and heroine into a crucible where they are held together and forced to confront feelings they would rather ignore.

These are, however, no more than frames.

Romantic fiction is character led. What brings readers back to our books time and time again is not the frame, the situation we have created to give our heroes and heroines a hard time. They come back for the emotion generated by those conflicts; the problems, heartaches that we toss in their path like so many hand grenades.

Our reader wants to experience what the hero or heroine is feeling. The excitement, the raised heart rate, the pounding pulse. An attraction that is all the more exciting, compelling, because it must be resisted.

For ten years he'd lived with a memory of her in his arms, the heavy silk of her hair trailing across his skin, her sweet mouth a torment of innocence and knowing eagerness as she'd taken him to a place that until then he hadn't known he wanted to go.

Lived with the memory of tearing himself away from her fully aware that he'd done the unforgivable then compounded his sin by leaving her asleep in his bed to wake alone.

He'd told himself that he had no choice.

Grace needed security, a settled home, a man who would put her first while, for as long as he could remember, he'd had his eyes set on far horizons, on travelling light, fast. That he needed total freedom to take risks as he built an empire of his own. — Secret Baby, Surprise Parents

The reader comes back for the internal battle. For the highs and lows. To have her withers rung by a black moment so dark that even when the heroine is proudly holding back her tears, they are running down her own cheeks and dripping onto the page.

...there was only one thing he longed for, yearned for. He hadn't known it, or particularly missed the lack of it, until this evening. But the ability to love one woman with all his heart and soul for the rest of life... That wasn't something that money could buy. — The Best Man & the Bridesmaid

The roller-coaster emotional thrill is what she demands in return for her trust in choosing your book out of the dozens laid out before her in the shop, in the library, on the internet. The emotion generated by conflicts, problems, heartaches that we toss in their path like so many hand grenades.

So where do you find that emotion?

Emotions are what make us human. They are the most simple and complex of feelings. They colour the way we see the world. They drive our actions for good or ill. They provoke tenderness or violence. Fight or flight.

They are simple because they are instinctive, intuitive, straight from the gut. You don't think or rationalise your emotions. You are overpowered by them, swept up by something raw, atavistic, beyond your control. True emotion is without artifice or deceit. It is honest.

She drew and drew and drew, ripping pages from her pad as she filled them, dropping them on the floor.

Images stored in her memory pouring out on the paper. She drew the garden from her window. The porch trailed with honeysuckle, her bike propped up against it.

The soft, warm rose and peach colours of the bricks of Wickham Lodge. The mock medieval turret. The wisteria, its thick twisted grey stems, long blue racemes echoed in the slate of the roof.

She drew a detail of the newel post, furniture she polished and knew as intimately as her own hand, the fold of the shawl over the sofa. She drew swift sketches of the people she worked for, producing, in a few lines a feature, a look, going back further and further until her slashing pastels produced Sean, lying in the road, the small hi-tech headphones still blaring out the blast of noise that had masked the sound of the approaching car. His hand resting against the bloodied headline proclaiming United's triumph in the League.

'How dare you!' she demanded. Slash, slash, slash. Her tears puddling in the red so that it ran into the black just as it had on that hideous day. 'How dare you be so careless. So thoughtless. How dare you die!' — The Secret Life of Lady Gabriella

What makes us laugh, what makes us cry, is deeply personal. It is who we are and can never be forced. It only works as part of our unconscious writing voice, something that comes naturally and your history will give you the tools you need.

This is what actors call "the method". Using those moments that stay with you; incidents – often small in themselves – that leave a lingering sense of outrage or pleasure. Those moments of excitement, helplessness, betrayal, embarrassment, joy that lodge in the mind and years later surface without warning, the feelings so vivid that you can still feel the hot blush.

Your reader wants to feel what the heroine is feeling. The roller-coaster emotional thrill is what she demands in return for her trust in choosing your book. That's the promise you have to deliver on.

Memory is the trigger. We are all sponges, soaking up images, sounds, feelings. As writers we have to tap into our own emotions and use them to create a living, breathing character.

At one point in *Tempted By Trouble*, hero and heroine are

laughing about the nosey, gossipy women in the village as Elle explains to Sean that each year, with the arrival of the Fair, she looks for a likeness, trying to spot the man who might be her father.

Sean's response — *'I think it's far more likely that some man would look up, see you with the sun shining on your hair and remember a long ago summer when he met a pretty girl. And wish he was still young...'* changes the mood from laughter to deep emotion in a heartbeat.

In romance you can have emotion without humour —
You cannot have humour without emotion.

Search your memory for an occasion when one moment you're laughing, on top of the world celebrating some achievement with family, friends and then, without warning, there's a prickle behind your eyelids. Present laughter evoking a memory that brings tears to your eyes before you know what happened.

What emotional trigger has caught you out that way?

- Making a birthday cake with your daughter and remembering doing the same thing with your own mother?
- Does seeing your husband put up the Christmas tree bring back good or bad memories?
- Being at a celebration and feeling the empty spaces left by loved ones who aren't there.

Bring your own experience to the table, use it to colour your writing, give power to your character's feelings.

The unspoken 'And you owe me...' lay unsaid between them. But she knew that, like her, he was remembering the hideous scene when he'd come to the back door, white-faced, clutching his roses. It had remained closed to his knock but he hadn't gone away. He'd stayed there, mulishly stubborn, for so long that her grandfather had told the gardener turn the hose on him.

It had been the week before Christmas and the water was freezing, but while he'd been driven from the doorstep, he'd stayed in the garden, defiantly, silently staring up at her room, visibly shivering, until it was quite dark.

She'd stood in this window and watched him, unable to do or say anything without making it much, much worse. Torn between her grandfather and the boy she loved. She would have defied her grandpa, just as her mother had defied him, but there had been Saffy. And Adam. And she'd kept the promise that had been wrung from her even though her heart was breaking.

She didn't owe him a thing. She'd paid and paid and paid...—
SOS: Convenient Husband Required

- She hurt.
- Her heart was breaking.
- It was like nothing she'd felt before.

We have all read those skim-over-the-surface sentences and felt cheated. If you find yourself writing anything like that, ask yourself:

- How is she hurting? What is special about her pain?
- What does her particular heartbreak feel like? Give her mental anguish real, physical properties.
- What is it that makes your heroine feelings unique?

Your reader wants to experience her emotional turmoil, her anguish, wants to feel her heart break. Don't write it in black and white, in two dimensions; give it shape, colour, texture. Make a scene of it. Write it in 3D Technicolor.

Use your senses to heighten the emotion. Because emotion is the key.

Josh held his breath, knowing that they were both on the precipice of something special. Keeping his eyes fixed firmly on her face. She was wearing something soft, silky with narrow straps and he slipped one over her shoulder, let his hand slide down over the full, soft mound of her breast where once her nipple had hardened eagerly for him, as if begging for his touch.

But this was not a girl's breast. Not the small, high breast, that tormented his dreams. It was a full, womanly, filled his hand as he lifted it, bent to kiss it.

'Please...'

'Anything,' he said, his eyes never leaving hers, 'you said you would do anything.' And seized by some atavistic need to make his own mark, he touched his tongue to her nipple.

It leapt in response and feeling like some great hunter bringing home food for his tribe, he offered it to his baby. — Secret Baby, Surprise Parents

If you can make a reader feel, you can make her smile. If you can make her smile, you can make her cry and if you can make her cry, you are a writer.

- Surprise your reader.
- Enchant her.
- Terrify her.
- Make her feel what you feel

CHAPTER FIVE

DEVELOPING THE ROMANCE THROUGH SEXUAL TENSION

Sexual tension is not just about getting naked. It's about wanting something and knowing it's out of reach. It can be a look instead of a touch.
   — Mollie Blake's Writing Workshop Notes from Secret Wedding by Liz Fielding

THE characters in a romance novel are, perhaps too often, the universally appealing tall, dark and handsome male, the girl with the heart-shaped face, long glossy hair, willowy figure. But that's not all they are. If that was all there is to them, how boring romance fiction would be. And it's not. Boring.

It's not that formulaic, either.

There's Donna Alward's wounded veteran hero in *Her Lone Cowboy* dealing with the loss of an arm.

There's India Grey's hero in *Mistress: Hired for the Billionaire's Pleasure*, who is losing his sight.

There's my own Matty in *The Marriage Miracle*, confined to a wheelchair following a road accident and Miranda, in *Wedded in a Whirlwind*, who has suffered a mental breakdown.

I've read romances with heroines who are living rough, have had problems with alcohol, and several who have been in jail — some unjustly, one guilty as charged. I've read a romance with a heroine who has killed her abusive husband, stories about women who have suffered the tragedy of still birth, the loss of a child.

Don't limit yourself by what you perceive to be the conventions of the genre. If you have a story burning to be told, don't hold back, but do focus on the emotional impact of what has happened to your character. Romantic fiction is entertainment and publishers are not looking for "issue" based books.

An upbeat ending is promised by the word "romance", just as justice is promised in crime fiction, or saving of the world in a thriller. In all genre fiction, readers come back again and again not for the destination, but for the journey.

There is certainly a framework to a classic romance — man/woman, attraction, conflict, despair, redemption, happy ending (Jane Austen set the standard and who's arguing) — but the uniqueness of the characters makes each romance different and the genre endlessly appealing.

You are not going to be writing a new story. What you will bring to the party will be a new voice, a fresh perspective, some unique view of life and love that is your own.

Your characters' journey might begin with an unexpected meeting with a stranger, or maybe the reunion of a couple who haven't met in a long time, or perhaps friends who are suddenly seeing one another in a new way, or as in *The Billionaire Takes a Bride,* with the heroine doing a spot of breaking and entering.

Light, she needed more light. As she reached for the lamp it came on by itself. Startled, she stared at it for a moment, then grinned. That was so brilliant! She'd heard of lamps that did that...

But this was not the time to investigate. She turned her attention back to the small metallic object she'd picked up. 'Oh, drat...'

'Not one of yours, I take it?'

The voice, low and gravelly had emerged from the heaped up quilt, along with a mop of dark, tousled hair and a pair of heavy lidded eyes. And a hand which was holding a remote...

It dropped the remote and reached out – it was attached to a sinewy arm she noticed—and lifted the sliver of platinum from her open palm, held it up against her ear, his warm fingers brushing against her neck.

Not a key, but an earring. Long, slender...

And that was just his fingers.

'No,' he said, after looking at it and then at her for what seemed like an age, during which her heart took a unilateral decision not to

beat – probably something to do with all the magnetism flowing from those electric blue eyes – before dropping it back into her hand. 'Not your style.'

However they meet, welcome or not, there will be an instant physical awareness. Let the reader see, feel that reaction.

It's not, of course, that simple. Boy meets girl, instant attraction, fall in love, live happily ever after is a delightful scenario, but it is not a story.

The initial attraction is only the first step along a path strewn with obstacles to love; issues of trust, control, fear and conflicting loyalties. After that first encounter, however, every thought, every move both hero and heroine make will be coloured by the memory of that attraction, those feelings.

Even as the tug of desire runs up against resistance when the "no way" defence mechanism kicks in, the next time your hero and heroine meet the effect of all that thinking will be to double the impact.

'This is the second time I've found you in my bedroom. Are you trying to tell me something?' He spoke with the cool assurance of man who'd been fending off eager women since puberty. Clearly convinced that this was simply another case of a pathetic woman flinging herself at him.

She knew he'd never believed in Hector…

Ginny, inwardly seething at being forced into such a position, swallowed her pride, dredged up a smile from the very depths of her soul and said, 'It looks bad, doesn't it?'

'The gossip columnists would have a field day,' he agreed. 'But if you don't tell them, I won't.'

He reached out a hand to help her to her feet.

Since her legs seemed incapable of managing this simple act for themselves, she took it. His fingers wrapped about her hand and for a moment neither of them moved. For a moment everything was so still that it felt as if time itself had stopped. — The Billionaire Takes a Bride

It is vital to have the hero and heroine on the page together for as much of the book as possible. They need time alone, a chance to develop an intimacy, but some of the time they will be constrained by the presence of others where every word they exchange will have a double meaning — one for those listening, one between themselves. This will lend an air of conspiracy to every word they speak, binding them together, two against the world.

If, as with *Tempted By Trouble*, there is a large cast, you can use the frustration of not being able to spend time together to raise the temperature; add a little creativity to the mix.

'You see how easy it is?' Sean said, and even though she couldn't see him she knew he was smiling.

'But I get to choose how it's served,' she went on, as if he hadn't spoken. 'Exactly where to pipe the ice cream…'

'Elle…' He wasn't laughing now.

'Where to drizzle the chocolate fudge sauce.' He uttered one word that assured her that she had his full attention. 'A special one made with coffee liqueur. I love coffee liqueur…'

'Excuse me, Miss Amery, but are we having phone sex?' he asked, his own voice pure Irish cream.

'Elle!' Geli yelled from the bottom of the stairs. 'I need you to look at what I've done.'

She sighed. 'With my family, it's the only kind we're ever likely to have.' — Tempted By Trouble

Each meeting, each thought, increases the awareness, raises the temperature, until the most casual of touches will be the equivalent of putting a light to the blue touch paper…

'Damn,' she said, as her hair collapsed untidily about her face and shoulders, digging around in her pocket to find another one, coming up empty handed. 'It really needs cutting.'

'No.' Sean's smile faded as he lifted a handful, letting it run through his fingers. 'Believe me, it really doesn't. It's perfect just the way it is.'

It was a gesture of such intimacy that for a moment Elle couldn't think, couldn't breath. Rooted to the spot, the only movement was the pulse beating in her neck, the rush of something irresistible sweeping through her veins. A weakness in her legs. The aching pull of desire for something that was unknown and yet as familiar as breathing.

There has to be danger in this increasing intimacy.

If there was no reason to resist the attraction, there would be no story.

Even for the most perfectly matched of couples, with no conflict issues, a lifetime bond involves giving up a part of self, yielding some individuality as they become one. In a romance, that surrender becomes magnified by personal history, loss, responsibility.

Each meeting, each touch will raise the stakes, increase the closeness, ramp up awareness until the tension is at breaking point.

The sexual tension, the sizzle in a romance is all about anticipation. Here, hero and heroine are in the hotel kitchen, dealing with an emergency, but as they work together, whipping up cake mix, the heat is still fizzing between them.

...he wasn't above wiping a finger round the bowl like a kid. She caught him red-handed, slapped him with a spoon and, instead of licking it himself, he offered it to her.

'Come on,' he said, tempting her. 'Tell me you can you resist.'

She looked up into hot liquid silver eyes and for a moment completely lost her head. She could not resist him. Not for a moment and closing her lips around his finger, she surrendered to the dizzying tug of desire and, as the sweetness melted on her tongue, she thought she'd pass out.

'Good?' he asked. And when she struggled to speak, 'Maybe I should try.' He didn't wipe his finger around the bowl, but lowered his head, touched his tongue to her lips. — Wedding at Leopard Tree Lodge

Here, the hero is waiting for the heroine when she comes back, hot and sweaty, looking her worst, from an early morning run.

'Wait...'

'What?'

He lifted a strand of damp hair from her cheek, tucked it behind her ear and then he cradled her face in his hands.

'Matteo, I'm...'

'Wait,' he said. And then he kissed her. Slow, thoughtful, it was

everything his last kiss had not been. Where that had been fire, this had a gradual, all-the-time-in-the-world warmth that had her toes curling with pleasure. When he finally lifted his head, he said, 'We missed our hello.'

'So we did.'

And she kissed him back, hopefully getting the same response from some part of him. Although her kiss had further to go to reach his toes. — Flirting With Italian

Language plays a big part in the sizzle of a romance, intensifying the closeness, adding richness to imagery, engaging the senses. As multi-award winning author, Barbara O'Neal describes it — layering on the lusciousness.

He held her with his body, with his eyes and the hot, sweet ache of desire surged through her veins, liquefied between her legs... — The Last Woman He'd Ever Date

It was as if their minds had touched, like a spark leaping a gap to complete an electrical circuit. — Wild Fire

Once the romance has been consummated you will lose a large part of the conflict unless the sex adds another layer of complication. Here, the hero discovers that a night with the heroine — in chapter one — has unavoidable consequences.

His hand was shaking as he reached for the piece of plastic with it's telltale line of blue. He gripped it hard, wrapping it in his fist, wanting to break it, smash it, make it go away. — The Bachelor's Baby

Love scenes in romantic fiction are not about body parts — or, as Jenny Haddon (*author Sophie Page*) describes them, "docking procedures".

Sex, for a woman, takes place in the six inches between her ears and the important word here is sensuality. Use language, images that heighten the sizzle factor for the reader.

The move exposed the delicious curve of neck and shoulder and all he could think about was touching his lips to the point where they met, about tasting her skin, sinking his teeth into the smooth flesh and sucking it into his mouth. — The Last Woman He'd Ever Date

Use the touch points of physical desire, emotional conflict and need to engage your heroine's mind as well as her heart; to call to something deep within your hero.

What is it about this man, this woman that changes everything? What will make the risk worthwhile?

...Elle was an emotional minefield. Best avoided, but if that was impossible, to be handled at long distance with the utmost caution.

He followed her through the living room expecting to find her stretched out on one of the chairs on the terrace. But no, typically she'd ignored the obvious option and was down on the dock, leaning back, propped up on her hands, face to the sun, shoes off and legs dangling over the edge. Invading his space and filling his head with images that he wouldn't be able to get out of his mind. That would stay with him, haunt him, torment him. — Tempted By Trouble.

Throughout the story, both hero and heroine will take steps forward in intimacy and then retreat, but with each move the bond between them will grow stronger.

How you show that will vary depending on the heat of the book you're writing. For a series like Harlequin Romance, your task, as a writer is to put them in close proximity at every possible opportunity, keep them within touching distance, turn up the heat and then prevent them from tearing each other's clothes off — or if they do, ensure that they do it behind closed doors.

Think of it as exquisitely sexy underwear. It's what you don't reveal that makes the image so seductive. You're selling the sizzle, not the steak.

For steamier romances, trust, understanding, knowledge will be built through physical intimacy, but in both instances the dance of advance and retreat will be the same as hero and heroine are forced to confront the need to lay bare their secrets, their innermost fears, their pain.

Lovage Amery had a smile to come home to. A voice that warmed him through, touching something buried so deep inside him that he hadn't known it was there. Even now was afraid to examine too closely for fear that it was an illusion.

She was a woman who had taken everything that life could throw at her and still took on emotional complications without reservations. No caveats or conditions. No ifs or buts...

No fear.

She had that from her mother, he suspected. It was the whole-hearted grasp on life that had somehow eluded him.

They were complete opposites in that. He'd taken a step back, determined not to break her heart, but he'd completely misunderstood her.

Elle might cling obsessively to physical security, but she gave love as if it came from a bottomless well. Would risk her heart without a second thought. While he was prepared to risk anything but. Hoarding his feelings like a miser, protecting them from danger, keeping them locked away until they were stunted, miserable things without value.

She was ready to come to his bed if he wanted her, and there was no doubt that he wanted her.

But forever?

How could you know, be sure? Or was that what she was telling him? That you couldn't ever be certain, but it was worth the risk anyway. — Tempted By Trouble

As the bond develops, so does trust, intimacy, the possibility of something lasting. When Sean drives half way across the country to find Elle's missing uncle the reader understands that he has become inescapably attached to her, even if he isn't yet ready to acknowledge the fact.

When she believes that he has left her to spend time with another woman, her pain shows that she is falling in love.

Their closeness when they are reunited is tender, special and having taken that step, moved to a point where the question is not "if" but "when" they will consummate their romance, the "black moment", when all the old uncertainties and fears rear up to undermine the newly discovered trust, will be like a knife in the gut.

They have risked everything and they have, it seems, lost. To come through this final challenge they will have to take a leap of faith, be bone-deep honest, hold nothing back.

It would be so easy to lie. So easy to say that he'd realised he was wrong and was coming back to save her. But only the truth would do. Everything that was in his heart. 'I stopped because I was so angry with you.'

'With me?'

'Oh, yes. I wanted to tear Frederickson apart with my bare hands, but it was you I was really angry with.' Once the flood gates were unlocked it all came pouring out of him. 'Angry with you for letting any man do that to you. For not valuing yourself. For not punching him in the eye the first time he'd come on to you.'

'That was the first...'

'For not punching him in the eye the first time he touched you, held onto your arm a little too long. I wanted to shake you, Elle, tell you that you were fool. Tell you that you are worth so much more than that. I wanted to shake you because you had made me believe and suddenly it was all falling apart. Shake you and hold you so that you'd know you never had to do that again. Hold you and tell you that I love you...' And he stopped. That was it. Those were the words. 'I love you.' — Tempted By Trouble

To develop the romance you need —

- instant attraction between your hero and heroine
- to keep them on the page together; constantly in each others thoughts when apart
- danger in increasing intimacy
- a constant advance and retreat closeness — two steps forward, one back
- commitment to be followed by a black moment
- a final scene in which hero and heroine lay themselves emotionally bare

To develop sexual tension you need —

- to raise physical awareness
- anticipation
- to engage all the senses

- unexpected meetings, phone calls, or texts to raise the heartbeat
- sensuous language

And ask yourself if you've made the most of every scene.

- Is something happening?
- Is there tension, conflict?
- Is the story moving forward?
- Does each chapter end with a moment that will make the reader turn the page and read on?

CHAPTER SIX

WRITE REALISTIC DIALOGUE

Use dialogue to move the story along. Use it to create tension, misunderstandings, to reveal character to the reader.
— Mollie Blake's Writing Workshop Notes from Secret Wedding by Liz Fielding

YOUR characters must speak to each other. A lot.

Dialogue will provide the heart of your story, it will comprise at least a third of your book, maybe more, certainly not less.

Most of it will be between the hero and the heroine. This is how the reader will get to know them, how they reveal themselves to each other. What they say — or don't say — and how they say it, lays bare character.

Well written dialogue adds sparkle and immediacy to a story, making the reader feel that she is involved, a part of the scene.

It provides the main constituents of drama:

- Pace
- Conflict
- Emotion

Realistic dialogue is not the same as the way people speak in the real world.

Next time you're in a restaurant or your office or the supermarket queue, listen to the way people talk to each other. (*Eavesdropping comes under the heading "Where I get my ideas from…"*) People talk over one another, they say "um" and "er", switch to something else mid sentence. This is especially so for long-time partners, or people who know one another very well and who, from long habit and intimate knowledge, effortlessly follow the thought switching.

In a novel — as in film, or your favourite TV soap opera — all those hesitations, deviations and repetitions are edited out.

Your heroine will not wander off the topic unless it's a plot device, or she realises that she's betraying herself, or is overcome with some intense emotion. When that happens, an "er" or an "um" or a sudden change of subject will have meaning to the reader.

The conversation between your hero and heroine will be witty, smart, crisp; they will, in other words, say what we might have said in the same circumstances, if only we had a day or two to polish every sentence, all the time in the world to construct a witty comeback, or a scathing put-down.

'Okay. Arms up.'
'No need for that. I've already surrendered...' Her voice died as he unfurled a tape measure. *'What are you going to do with that?'*
He lifted his brows imperceptibly, inviting her to use her imagination. — The Bridesmaid's Reward

- Keep it short. Don't use ten words when five will do.
- Keep it believable. Use words that fit your character.
- Start a new paragraph whenever a new character speaks.

Conversation in the real world often has little point to it. It's mostly about the commonplace of existence. In a novel, however, it should have a purpose. It should advance the plot, move the story forward, tell us something about the characters who are speaking.

For the purpose of storytelling, you will need to cut out most of the small stuff. Obviously you want your conversations to sound natural, but your characters have to get to the point rather more quickly than we generally do in real life.

'Tell me, Jane, would you settle for a platonic marriage?'
This was it. The opening she'd been waiting for. She swallowed. 'Are you asking me?' she replied, her voice perfectly calm even while her heart was pounding loud enough to be heard in the next county.

'Yes,' he said. 'I want to know if you'd marry a man who wasn't in love with you.'

She shook her head. More hair slithered from the grip of pins unequal to the task. 'No, Mark. That wasn't my question.' He frowned, and she very nearly lost her nerve. It wasn't too late to bottle out... 'My question was...are you asking me if I'd marry you?'

— The Perfect Proposal

Dialogue should —

- change the character's situation
- throw light on what the character wants
- move the story forward

Dialogue also provides information and back story — in bite-sized chunks. The last thing the reader wants is a speech from one of the characters, or an information dump from the author. She wants short, pithy exchanges. Here, the hero, suffering from the after-effects of malaria, wakes to find the heroine in bed with him.

'You, um, had a fever,' I said, in an attempt to distract myself. Well I had to say something. 'You were shivering.'

'Is that right? And is this some new treatment that hasn't made it into the textbooks?'

There was a hint of something teasing in his voice, but like the smile it was buried deep. I was prepared to dig...

'It was an emergency,' I pointed out. 'This seemed like the most energy efficient way of dealing with the situation.'

'Energy efficient?'

That one nearly got him. He was having to work at not smiling now. Encouraged I said, 'It's called heat transfer.'

'I thought that was something to do with plumbing.'

Close...

'You're thinking of heat exchange.'

'I am?' He sounded surprised that I would know the difference. Well, heck I was a blonde...

'I worked as a receptionist at a heating and ventilation company for a while.' A very short while. One of the directors was very keen to explain all about heat exchange one night. After the office closed.

'Oh, please, don't misunderstand me. I'm not complaining. This is much more, um, efficacious than being manhandled into an ambulance by a couple of burly paramedics and carted off to hospital.'

Efficacious?

Oh, no. I wasn't going to smile until he did. Close thing, though.

I cleared my throat, giving myself a moment to get my face under control. 'Actually, I did think about calling them.' Well, I had. Momentarily. Until I realised I'd have to go downstairs to use the phone. 'But since you'd undoubtedly refuse to go with them for the second time in as many days, I decided I'd just get arrested for serially time-wasting the emergency services' over-stretched resources. I'm much too busy for that.'

'Doing what?'

He sounded genuinely interested. I suspected he was applying the same distraction technique...

'Finding a proper job...' — *as opposed to an improper one where I ended up lying in bed with my boss* — *'...preferably in the next twenty-four hours. Finding somewhere to live, ditto. Then there's walking your dogs twice a day. Oh, and cleaning a flower shop in the evening.'*

'Busy schedule. And you've still found time to make it your personal responsibility to be my guardian angel.'

I didn't feel like an angel, but clearly it would not be in my best interests to tell him that. Probably. But with a name like Gabriel he would know more about it than me. — A Surprise Christmas Proposal

And yes, there are two "ums" in that exchange. In the first, the heroine is dealing with an "oh heck!" moment. In the second, the hero is teasing the heroine by repeating it back at her.

Dialogue should —

- tell you about the character
- tell you about the relationship between the hero and heroine
- be entertaining

When you reveal the big emotional blockage that is preventing this couple from accepting their future, never write it as introspection — the examination of one's own thoughts — or allow the heroine to tell her best mate, or to write it in a letter.

These are the toughest scenes to write, but that is because they so important. They reveal the heart of a character. They expose your hero or heroine to ridicule, rejection, even revulsion. It requires all their courage, a giant leap of faith, to share their secrets, their fears with someone whose good opinion they really care about, with someone they love.

When your heroine tells her hero about something in her past that changed her life, that caused her immense pain or guilt, it is dialogue's big moment.

If you're struggling with it, try and imagine that it's your story. Imagine that you're telling it someone you care about, whose opinion matters to you. Say it out loud onto tape if you can. There'll be loads of "ers" and "ums" and pauses, but when you've transcribed it, cleaned it up, taken out every last unnecessary word, it will have great power.

'You were pregnant?' That stopped him. She'd known it would.

'My last throw of the dice. I thought if I had his baby a man wouldn't ever be able to leave me. Stupid. Unfair. Irresponsible beyond belief.'

'People do crazy things when they're unhappy,' he said.

'No excuses, Nick. Using a child...' She shrugged. 'Of course he insisted I terminate the pregnancy and, well, I've already told you that I'd have done anything...'

'Where is this child now?'

'You're assuming I didn't go ahead with it.' How generous of him. How undeserved...

'Are you saying you did?'

They were lying quite still but when, beside her, Nick Jago stopped breathing, it felt as if the world had stopped.

'The decision was taken out of my hands, Nick. I was crossing the road to the clinic when I collapsed. The driver did his best to avoid me, but I didn't even look before I stepped off the kerb.'

And with that everything started again. His breathing. Her heart...

'Were you badly injured?'

'A few bumps and bruises. I got off lightly.' She swallowed. 'By the time my brother made it back from wherever he was I was home and it was all over. Nothing to make a fuss about.'

'You didn't tell him, did you?'

'I think that was what worried Ivo most,' she said. 'The fact that I didn't make a fuss.'

'You lost your baby and didn't tell anyone?'

'He already had the world on his shoulders. He didn't need me as well. And I was so ashamed...'

'But you didn't do anything.'

'I thought about it, Jago ...' — Wedding in a Whirlwind

- Use dialogue to reveal back story through a moment of great emotional tension.
- Use dialogue to heat up the action, put a little sizzle into the mix.

'It won't be hard work, I promise you.'

His low honeyed voice promised her all kinds of things, none of them arduous, and as he picked up her hand the heat intensified.

'We can begin with something simple.' And never taking his eyes from her face, he touched his lips to the tip of her little finger. 'Wahid.'

'Wahid?'

'One.'

'Ithnan.' His lips moved on to her ring finger, lingered while she attempted to hold her wits together and repeat the word.

'Ithnan. Two.'

'Thalatha.'

Something inside her was melting and it took her so long to respond that he began to nibble on the tip of her middle finger.

'Thalata!'

'Arba'a.' And he drove home the message with four tiny kisses on the tip, the first joint, the second joint, the knuckle of her forefinger.

'Arba'a.' It was her bones that were the problem, she decided. Her bones were melting. That was why she couldn't move. Pull free. 'Four.'

'Khamsa.' He looked for a moment at her thumb, then took the length of it in his mouth before slowly pulling back to the tip. 'Five.'

— *Her Desert Dream*

- Use dialogue to reveal character.

As each character will look different, they will sound different, too. Men and women use different words to express the same things. Education, age, background will colour vocabulary.

A teenager will speak very differently from an adult; a teenager will not use the same language when speaking to an adult that she uses when speaking to her contemporaries. While teens do use slang, this will date very quickly so don't get carried away with it; it will probably be history before your book is published.

Men will speak differently to each other than to a woman or a child.

A man, revealing his inner feelings, will find it painful. He won't say that he's hurting, or that it's difficult; it will be revealed in his speech pattern.

'She was always very kind to me. I missed her when she left.' She looked at him, but his expression gave nothing away. 'After your father died.'

His mouth tightened. 'It was an accident waiting to happen. The towpath on a foggy night is no place for a drunk.'

'Hal...' she warned, with a touch to his arm, reminding him that they weren't alone. Curling her fingers back when he looked across at her. 'I'm sorry. I didn't know. About your Dad.'

'Why would you? You were never around when he came home after closing time.'

'No.' Had he been a violent drunk, or a sullen one? She restrained a shiver. 'Even so it was a shocking thing.'

'Why don't you say what's really on your mind, Claire? Where was I when my mother needed me?'

'No... At least I assumed the ban was still in place,' she said. 'I begged my mother to speak to Sir Robert. It seemed so cruel.'

'Did you?'

Was that a smile? Stupid question, her heart rate had gone through the roof...

'And did she?'

She shook her head. 'She said I didn't understand. That it wasn't

that simple. That you'd never come back.'
'How wrong can you get?' — The Last Woman He'd Ever Date

Men tend to speak in shorter sentences, use less emotional language than women. Use fewer words. It doesn't mean they don't feel things as deeply.

SPEECH TAGS

The purpose of speech tags — "he said", "she said" — is to ensure the reader knows who is speaking. You do not have to use them on every occasion.

This is a moment when my hero and heroine are in a car and the conversation is fast flowing, intense, with layers of meaning and the last thing you want is to distract the reader with a lot of tags.

Taking her silence for agreement, he said, 'You're a local reporter, aren't you?'
'Not much of one according to you.'
'You've sharpened up your act since then.'
'I took your advice, Hal. Nothing personal.'
'I think Mr Mean is about as personal as it gets, Claire. The fact that you haven't been back to see Archie and asked Gary to deliver your cake, suggests that you're aware of that.'
'I told you, I've been busy. There's so much to do in the garden at this time of year.'
'I know. The contractor is going to be clearing the rose garden next week.'
'Hal!'
He said nothing.
'Didn't you contact any of the rose specialists I sent you?'
'I've been busy. I have a company to run, as well as a house to restore.'
'And motorcycles to play with.'
'That too.'
'I'll do it for you—'
'Not unless you can wave your magic wave. You're going to be far too busy granting other people's wishes to work on your own.' — The Last Woman He'd Ever Date

In the following exchange, the hero and heroine have only just met and the dialogue is quieter, does not have the swift cut and thrust of the previous example. In this instance the speaker is introduced with an identifying action. On the fourth exchange, "she shook her head" is used to ensure that the reader keeps up with the exchange. In the fifth, "He glanced at her neighbour" again identifies the speaker without the use of a tag. In the sixth comes the first "she said".

He reached up and took the photograph from the shelf, then turned to Violet Hamilton and with the slightest of bows, said, 'Will you come to Ras al Kawi with me, princess? Bring the khanjar home?'

'Princess! Oh, please...'

'The daughter of a sheikha is a sheikha. As a direct descendant of Fatima, the title is yours by right.'

She shook her head, emphatically. 'No.'

'It's the truth and I am inviting you to see for yourself where you come from, to learn your history. To return the Blood of Tariq and place it where it belongs, in the hand of my grandfather.' He glanced at her neighbour, then back at Violet. 'In Ras al Kawi I can offer protection from those who would stop at nothing to use you.'

Use her? How? She was nobody...

'I ... I can't,' she said. 'I can't just up sticks and go to Ras al...'

'Kawi. Ras al Kawi.'

'Ras al Kawi.' She repeated the name as if it echoed, like some precious tribal memory, deep in her heart.

'If you are not here, they cannot use you. Or threaten your friends to get what they want.'

'They wouldn't!' she exclaimed. Then realised that they already had. 'What do they want?'

'Power,' he said. — Chosen As the Sheikh's Wife

Again, I advise the study of writers whose work you admire and enjoy reading. See what techniques they use to keep you connected. You will often find quite long sections of dialogue with hardly a tag in sight.

When you do need a tag, however, there really is nothing to beat the basic "he said", "she said".

Dialogue littered with adverbs — he growled, grumbled, laughed; she tittered, shrieked, called — becomes ridiculous, tedious. Use them sparingly. On reflection, I didn't need the "exclaimed" tag in the previous passage. I'd used an exclamation mark, which was enough.

With speech tags, less is definitely more.

If you need to describe the way someone has spoken, or show what they're feeling as they speak, if is often better to use a separate sentence. What they do, or think, will give you the subtext far more effectively than an adverb stuck onto a tag.

'Actually, I'm not the only one around here with an interesting nose.' Her voice was too bright, her attempt at a laugh forced. 'Yours has been broken...' — Wedded in a Whirlwind

'Done! We're far from done!' Sir Robert Cranbrook clutched at the table, hauled himself to his feet. 'Your mother was a cheating whore who took the money...' — The Last Woman He'd Ever Date

TO SUM UP DIALOGUE SHOULD —

- Be crisp, concise
- Flow; read effortlessly
- Drive the plot forward
- Reveal character
- Add conflict
- Provide information and fill in back story
- Add pace, sizzle, emotion
- Entertain

CHAPTER SEVEN

VIEWPOINT

Whose story are you telling? Whose head are you in, whose eyes are you seeing through?
— Mollie Blake's Writing Workshop Notes by Liz Fielding

WHEN you begin your book you must decide who is going to be your major viewpoint character. This is best decided by asking yourself who, in your book, has most at stake? Whose shoes will the reader be walking in?

THIRD PERSON, PAST TENSE

There was a time, when I first started writing romance for Harlequin Mills and Boon, when there was no decision to make. Your viewpoint character would be the heroine and no one else. This was her story and it would be told in the third person, past tense.
This is from my first book.

'I hope it was insured.' Her father's wry comment gave her pause. She hadn't expected him to be pleased with her. But it wasn't like him to be so angry. He was mostly amused by the scrapes she got into in pursuit of one cause or another.
She tried to rouse him to her side. — An Image of You

I have read books where the author appears to distrust the reader's ability to keep up with who is speaking. Here's the same excerpt written this way.

'I hope it was insured.' Her father's wry comment gave Georgette pause. Georgette hadn't expected him to be pleased with her. But it wasn't like her father to be so angry. Her father was mostly amused by the scrapes she got into in pursuit of one cause or another.
Georgette tried to rouse her father to her side...

This has the effect of leaving the reader with the feeling they are being beaten around the head with the character names. It's Georgette — bang, talking to her father — bang.

Don't do it. If there are two people in a room talking to one another, the reader will keep up, I promise.

One of the problems with third person, single viewpoint is that short of using some device such as a mirror — so clichéd — it's difficult for the writer to describe the heroine, since the reader is in her head for the entire book.

Moments when the heroine tossed back her "abundant red/ebony/fair hair" are frequent —and understandable — in older books, but no one thinks of themselves in that way and it's a very dated style. This is from an early book of mine —

Sophie eased her shoulder, pushed back a wayward strand of fair hair that had escaped her plait to cling clammily to her forehead and watched her quarry, now slicing relentlessly through the water. —
Prisoner of the Heart

Obviously we don't think about the colour of our hair in that way — although the plait usefully tells us that Sophie's hair is long — but back then we all did it.

MULTIPLE VIEWPOINT

With multiple viewpoint this is no longer a problem, we have the hero to fill in all the gaps in a much more satisfactory way and to compare the heroine's vision of herself with the one the hero is seeing. *(She sees fat, he sees voluptuous!)*

Do, however, always be aware of whose head you're in at any given time and what they can and — more importantly — cannot know or see.

It was like flinging off tightly-laced corsets when I wrote my first book for HMB using dual viewpoint, allowing the reader to see into the head, the heart, of the hero, but still in third person, past tense. That is, with few exceptions, the way most books are now written for this publisher.

This works especially well in romance.

Including both the hero and heroine viewpoints gives insight into both sides of the developing relationship. It also creates and maintains suspense and conflict because the writer is able to cut away from one character to another at a pivotal moment, creating a cliff-hanger effect.

He clung to the edge of the sink, reminding himself that she was pregnant. That whatever she was doing, for whatever reason, her baby had to come first.

And he turned on the tap but instead of filling the kettle, he scooped up handfuls of water, burying in face in it to cool the heat of lips that still tasted of her.

And then, when that didn't help, ducking his head beneath the icy water.

Sylvie abandoned her burden on the library table and gave herself up to the comfort of one of the old leather wing-chairs pulled up by the fire and closing her eyes, but more in despair than pleasure.

The intensity of the attraction had not diminished, that much was obvious. It wasn't just her, it was a mutual connection, something beyond words, and yet it was as if there was an unseen barrier between them.

Or perhaps it was the all too visible one. — The Bride's Baby

To go deeper in the third person point of view, intensify the emotional bond between the viewpoint character and the reader, it helps to avoid reflection.

She *wondered* if he would return.
Would he return?

She *decided* to clean the house.

Scrubbing helped. She scrubbed, scoured, polished...

She *felt* hot.
Her fingers were sticking to the keyboard. Sweat was running down her back...

Deep third helps to pull the reader into the story, experience it through the character's eyes, through her feelings, both physical and emotional.

FIRST PERSON, PAST TENSE

The use of third person, past tense, is not, however, written in viewpoint stone, even for the most classic of romances published by Harlequin Mills and Boon. I have written two books using first person, from the heroine's point of view.

'Are you sure you don't want to take this sweater, Philly? Aunt Alice will expect to see you wearing it at Christmas...' My mother looked up when I didn't answer and caught me looking at the quiz in the magazine she'd bought me on her last-minute dash to shops. 'Save that for the journey, dear,' she said, as if I were six years old, instead of nearly twenty-three, 'or you won't have anything to read on the train.' — City Girl in Training

'What kind of job are you looking for, Miss Harrington?'
'Please, call me Sophie. Peter always does.'
And where was Peter when I needed him? I'd been bringing my untapped potential to this employment agency for the last five years...— A Surprise Christmas Proposal

Writing these two books was enormous fun, but there are downsides to first person. The reader cannot experience what the hero is feeling, or know what he's thinking. And some readers don't like it — I know this because a couple of them wrote and begged me not to do it again. If your story demands it, however, go ahead. *A Surprise Christmas Proposal* is amongst my best selling books so a lot of people must have enjoyed it.

FIRST PERSON PRESENT TENSE

Present tense is mostly the territory of chick-lit novels such as the Shopaholic series by Sophie Kinsella and some crime fiction. Here's a brief excerpt from *Her Wish-List Bridegroom* first as it appeared in the book and then in first person present tense.

She called at the job agency first, filled in the form they produced, sat while the woman behind the desk glanced over her qualifications, the steady advancement with her only employer since university.

'You haven't answered the question about why you left your last employer.'

'No.' Well, that was a tricky one. 'Sorry.' She took the form and wrote "Bridget Jones Syndrome" and pushed it back across the desk.

'You shagged your boss?'

'No, I was the boss, but you know how it is with men. They always want to be on top.'

I call at the job agency first, fill in the form they produce, sit while the woman behind the desk glances over my qualifications, the steady advancement with my only employer since university.

'You haven't answered the question about why you left your last employer.'

'No.' Well, that was a tricky one. 'Sorry.' I take the form and write "Bridget Jones Syndrome" then push it back across the desk.

'You shagged your boss?'

'No, I was the boss, but you know how it is with men. They always want to be on top.'

Present tense does lend immediacy to the action and if it feels right for your story, go for it.

SWITCHING VIEWPOINT

Some writers insist that there should only be one viewpoint in one chapter. Some are less prescriptive and say that there should only be one viewpoint per scene. Some writers ignore this rule completely — most famously, best-selling author, Nora Roberts.

In early books, with only heroine viewpoint, I did not have to confront this issue. When I wrote *Eloping With Emmy,* my first dual viewpoint book for Harlequin Mills and Boon, however, I began with a scene that switched rapidly between Tom (downstairs in the study with Gerald Carlisle) and Emmy Carlisle (locked in the upstairs nursery and doing her best to escape). I used the movie technique, switching between the scenes as they got closer and closer until there was the inevitable confrontation.

I could not have written that scene without switching viewpoint within the chapter.

Later, writing *Dating Her Boss,* there was a moment where, for the first time, I consciously shifted viewpoint within a scene. The hero and heroine were dancing. It was a pivotal scene and I wanted the reader to experience what each of them was feeling as it happened, when they were in each other's arms, in the heat of the moment, rather than with one of them thinking about it later.

Richie? Who in their right mind would be thinking about Richie at a moment like this? Jilly pulled herself together. 'Richie won't notice.'

'Oh, he will. He has.' Max, a head taller than Jilly could see him now...

The vital thing with a switch mid-scene is to keep the reader with you, never let her flounder for a moment.

Here the switch is immediate, the viewpoint shifting with the pattern of the dance.

It is simpler if you can use a natural break, a pause in a conversation, or when some outside agency, such as a dog, or child, or telephone breaks the intensity of the scene.

'I'm actually making tea,' she continued, in an effort at appeasement. After all she had not only matched his rudeness, but trumped it. 'However, while acknowledging your undoubted competence, it would be no trouble to make you a pot of coffee at the same time. Since I'm boiling the kettle anyway. You can come back when I've gone upstairs and help yourself if you don't want to stay.'

There was a moment of absolute silence when the air was thick with words waiting to be spoken. Not even the dog moved.

Harry felt as if his feet were welded to the floor. His brain was urging him to walk out. He couldn't handle people. Couldn't handle this woman who one minute was all soft curves and temptation and the next, disapproval and a sharp tongue. — A Nanny for Keeps

This is all about technique and can be learned — again study your favourite authors and see what they do — but for the beginning writer I would suggest sticking to one viewpoint per scene. It's not a rule, it's just simpler and you're less likely to get into a muddle. Where — if — you choose to switch within scenes is a personal choice, part of your writing voice, your style but, however you approach it, always ensure that the reader knows whose eyes she's seeing through, whose thoughts she's privy to.

- Choose your viewpoint to suit your genre
- The reader can only see through the viewpoint character's eyes
- The reader can only be privy to the viewpoint character's thoughts
- Ensure that viewpoint changes are seamless for the reader
- Use viewpoint change to create a cliff-hanger moment

CHAPTER EIGHT

CONSTRUCT A FOUR DIMENSIONAL WORLD

You touch and see in three dimensions. The fourth dimension is the ephemeral. The stuff you hear, smell, taste. Use all the senses.
—Mollie Blake's Writing Workshop Notes by Liz Fielding

THE place your characters inhabit should be glimpsed in the opening so that the reader is grounded in their world.

The important word in that sentence is "glimpsed".

I once read a book written by a bestselling thriller writer. In the opening scene the hero, a writer, visits his agent's office. Every detail of that office is described. The decoration, the layout of the furniture, how he walked from reception to the office of the man he had come to see. It was a desperately dull opening but I stuck with it because (a) I trusted the author to deliver and (b) it was a thriller and I assumed that this was the set up for some later "big scene" when all these details would become vital.

The hero never went back to the office.

I have no way of knowing if the author had planned a big scene set there later in the book and changed his mind, or was simply writing himself into the hero's head and forgot to cut it.

The setting is a backdrop to the action; it should underpin it, not overwhelm it.

A snapshot, a brief, thumbnail sketch will allow each reader to fill in the details from her own mental picture gallery and see it clearly in her mind's eye. Make it her own.

- *The Assembly Rooms were straight out of a Jane Austen*

novel. Georgian and decaying grandly in the manner of some great old actress, with charm and elegance. — His Personal Agenda

- *...the journey gave them a fairy-tale view of the city from the lake, the floodlit castle, layer upon layer of lights descending and then reflected back in the ripples. — The Valentine Bride*

- *Steps led up to a piazza, golden in the sunlight, shaded with trees. There were small shops, a café where the aproned proprietor was setting out tables and a church that seemed far too large for such a small place. — Flirting With Italian*

Use all of your senses, not just sight.
A large part of one of my books, takes place in total darkness.

In the intensity of the silence, she could have sworn she heard the creak of muscle as his face creased into the grin. A grin that she could hear in his voice as he said, 'Tough little thing, aren't you?'

And in spite of everything she was grinning herself as she said, 'You have no idea.'

For a moment they knelt in that close circle with every sense intensified by the darkness, aware of each other in ways that only those deprived of sight can ever be.

The slight rise and fall of Jago's chest, the slow, steady thud of his heartbeat through her palm.

She could almost taste the pulsing heat of his body. — Wedded in a Whirlwind

To escape from the rock tomb where they have been imprisoned by an earthquake, Manda and Jago have to put total trust in one another. They learn to do that through touch and scent and the subtleties of inflection as they speak that would normally have escaped them. The intensity of the hours they spend together, facing the possibility of death at any moment, are heightened by the darkness.

Don't overload the reader with sensory images, however. You don't need everything. One or two are sufficient, even in a scene, like this one, packed with action.

The jolting tango along the black bulk of the Landcruiser, the bruising jerk as her seat-belt locked and bit into her shoulder, the airbag exploding into life. The final nightmarish sound of rending metal as she collided with the hangar. — Wild Lady

The world is a noisy place so don't forget to give your story a soundtrack. Think about where your characters are. Stand for a moment in a supermarket and listen the layers of sounds. The buzz of voices, the sound of a barcode reader, the clink of cash, music, the shout of a child, a Tannoy announcement.

Stand in your scene and ask yourself what your characters will hear.

- *There were lights everywhere, a brass band was playing Christmas carols as crowds of shoppers searched out presents for people they loved.— Christmas Angel for the Billionaire*

- *Strong fingers teased the keys, tormenting the mellow sound that spiralled upwards, soaring dangerously higher and higher until Rosalind caught her breath on a top note held endlessly, balancing on the razor-edge of destruction. — Dangerous Flirtation*

- *The rustling grew louder. It was above them, around them, the air stirring and suddenly he knew what it was. 'Flora!' he warned, as she raised her camera to take a picture. 'Don't!' — The Marriage Merger*

What can your characters smell? Is there a bakery nearby? A burger van? Are there diesel fumes? Wet dog? Wet baby?

- *She could feel every move he made, every breath and even the familiar smell of hot oil from the engine of the aged Land Rover couldn't mask the scent of warm male. — Christmas Angel for the Billionaire*

- *There was a sweet fresh green scent from the grass that reached out across the sparse bush that drew the animals from across the Kalahari, especially now as they neared the end of the dry season. — Wedding at Leopard Tree Lodge*

• *...some subtle scent that reminded her of a long ago walk in autumn woods. The crushed dry leaves and bracken under foot. —*

Add texture to your story. How do things feel? Cloth, soap, skin, the sugary doughnut against the heroine's lips. A hot cup warming cold hands.

• *Rubble rattled off her as she finally managed to sit up; small pieces of stone along with what felt like half a ton of fine cloying dust that rose up to choke her. — Wedded in a Whirlwind*

• *She gingerly eased herself onto her shoulder, then gave a little gasp at the unexpected intimacy of his cold fingers against the sensitive, nylon-clad flesh as he hooked his hand beneath her knee. — The Last Woman He'd Ever Date*

• *Beneath his fingers he could feel her pulse throbbing at her temple. The edge of his thumb brushing against her cheekbone raised the fine down as she shivered against him, as if every minute contact of his skin against hers was an agony of pleasure. — Wild Justice*

Think about taste. Use it to add depth to the sensations that are bombarding your character, to bring your reader into the story.

• *The grape exploded on her tongue, the juice dribbling over her lips, over his fingers. And it seemed the most natural thing in the world to lick it up...— Flirting With Italian*

• *...all she could taste was the acid of the few sips of champagne she had swallowed after the jump as she wretched and wretched and then slumped on the floor, her back against the bath, her cold clammy forehead on her knee. — Wild Lady*

• *'Don't you sometimes long for a taste of rice pudding the way your mother made it? With butter and sultanas and freshly grated nutmeg?' — Gentlemen Prefer ... Brunettes*

To sum up, remember —

- a glimpse of setting is enough, allow the reader to fill in the details using her own imagination
- use all of the senses — but not all at the same time
- use broad brush strokes to give an impression
- highlight tiny details to add intensity

CHAPTER NINE

GIVE THE READER A SATISFYING ENDING

A satisfying ending provides a final moment of discord before all the loose ends are gathered in, with reassurance that the hero and heroine will live happily ever after.
— from Mollie Blake's Writing Workshop Notes from Secret Wedding by Liz Fielding

WHILE the grab-your-throat opening your have created will sell your book, it is the ending that will sell the next one.

Your ending should leave the reader with a sigh of satisfaction, a longing for more. Most of all, the reader should close the book feeling that the hero and heroine have been tested, that they have faced their darkest fears and come shining through.

They should have grown in stature during the journey they began on page one and deserve their happy ever after.

You need to plant the seeds of your ending early in the book.

If your heroine hates her job, what career will make her happy? There could be a clue in what she does for pleasure. How will that tie in with her growth during the story, the confidence she gains?

* *'Rosie is a bit too old for that kind of excitement,' he said. 'She's available for events, though. Parties. Weddings.'* — *Tempted By Trouble*

Here is a foreshadowing of the solution to Elle's problems — running an event business using this unwelcome gift of a vintage ice cream van.

- *'It breaks my heart to see the garden in this state,' she said, sipping at her tea. 'It makes my fingers itch to get stuck in with the sécateurs. — The Last Woman He'd Ever Date*

Here Claire is voicing what she really wants to do with her life long before she understands it herself.

- *'If you want the unadorned truth,' she said, 'I hate my career, I hate my marriage—-' — Reunited: Marriage in a Million*

Belle does not hate her husband — she is passionately in love with him — only a marriage that is build on a lie. To find her happy ending she has to look her past squarely in the face, deal with her guilt, heal old wounds and, in doing so, she discovers that she is not the only one in her marriage with dark secrets.

To discover their happy ending each of these women will have to surrender the security they crave and accept their true destiny, but that destiny cannot come out of the blue. The ending of your book should grow organically from your characters and their internal conflicts. It will be the ending your hero and heroine were heading for from the beginning.

It will not be easy but, as your reader finishes your story, closes the book, it should feel inevitable. Right.

The ending must resolve the central conflict of the story. All secrets revealed, an acceptance of loss, a belief in a shared future.

Both hero and heroine must have shaken off the darkness that is keeping them from moving forward. Even if — heaven forbid — their romance was a short-lived affair, they would both still have gained from knowing each other. They will have become the people they have the potential to be.

Do you remember Joan Wilder in the film *Romancing the Stone?* At the beginning of the film she is terrified of her own shadow; by the end we see her striding down the street, talking to her neighbours, full of confidence, and when her agent declares her to be a "world class hopeless romantic", she says "no, I'm a world class *hopeful* romantic". And she doesn't hesitate when her lover returns but climbs aboard his yacht, ready for the adventure that awaits her.

It's important to tie up all the loose ends, even the smallest sub plot. In one of my books the heroine discovers that she's been adopted. The secrecy causes a rift between her and her adoptive mother and Louise contacts her birth mother, the flighty Patsy. In the final scene, at the wedding, the two women come face to face.

- *And there was Patsy.*
She came in last with her new husband and Louise kissed them both, then turned to her mother and said, 'Mummy, may I introduce Patsy Simpson Harcourt and her husband Derek? Patsy, this is my mother. — The Valentine Bride

She has found her birth mother, made friends with her, but on this most important day, she acknowledges the woman who raised her, who was there for her every day of her life, as her real mother.

Be creative with your ending. It should belong to your characters, evolving out of their story.

Maybe the arrival of a much wanted baby would be the perfect ending. Or the adoption of a child. Or a reunion with someone who has been lost. Or maybe the hero or the heroine will create some especially inventive scenario for a proposal.

Here the heroine is working as a check-out girl in a supermarket and the hero — who has been watching her unnoticed, seen her many small kindnesses as she helps harassed mothers, the elderly, despite her evident exhaustion — steps forward and places a ring on the conveyor belt, choosing to make a very public statement of his love for her.

- *He saw her gather herself for one last effort. Put the smile back in place, turn to wait for the goods to reach her. Saw the smile falter, the frown buckle her brow as she watched the tiny dark blue, velvet covered box move slowly towards her. The diamond solitaire at its heart spark a rainbow of light. — Her Desert Dream*

A fabulous wedding is always fun and is a great place to tie up all the loose ends, a time for reconciliation, renewal. Do try to bring something fresh to the celebrations, however, some personal touch from the book — some small thing that shows how in touch with each other your hero and heroine are, a demonstration that they've been paying attention.

The hero who chooses ducks instead of doves for his bride's wedding.

The hero who flies to the other side of the world to bring a long lost foster mother to the wedding.

A hero who moves heaven and earth to make a vital wedding deadline for his heroine.

Think about your characters. Ask yourself what would make the day extra special for them. A glimpse of the future always goes down well, too.

- Foreshadow the ending early in the story
- The ending should grow organically from the characters
- Be creative with the proposal, the wedding
- Remember that the end of the book is not the end of your hero and heroine's story — your reader should be able to envision the life they will live when she's closed the book.

CHAPTER TEN

THE BASICS

Agents and editors are busy people. Make it easy for them to love your book. Sweat the small stuff — the spelling, the grammar, a professional looking manuscript.
  —from Mollie Blake's Writing Workshop Notes by Liz Fielding

GRAMMAR

GRAMMAR — commas, full stops, apostrophes, spelling — are the nuts and bolts of writing. They make what we write intelligible to the reader.

I'm not a great grammarian. I use language in ways that serve my story. If I want single word sentences, I'll use them. If I want a sentence without a verb, I'll do that, too — but not too often. No doubt like mine, your computer throws up wiggly underlining when it finds something of which it disapproves.

Mostly, in my case, it will be because I've written a "fragment" rather than a proper sentence. I'll take a look and sometimes I'll rethink what I've written, combine two sentences if it makes more sense for the reader.

Sometimes I'm surprised to discover that I can't spell a word when I thought I could and I'm grateful for the help. Sometimes it will be querying my use of an apostrophe. *(It's asking me to think about it, not telling me I've got it wrong - it just sees an apostrophe and thinks "Uh-oh"...)*

Do you know the difference between "its" and "it's"?

The thing is it really *matters*.

In a world where editors and agents struggle for every minute in their day, they no longer have the time to bother with someone who hasn't taken the trouble to master the basic skills of writing a sentence.

Read your work out loud and you'll soon see the importance of proper punctuation. The good news is that anyone can learn this stuff. I'm not talking about the strange words — gerunds and past participles — but the reason for using an apostrophe and how commas help make sense of a sentence.

We all race through a rattling good yarn without noticing the punctuation. That's the point. Punctuation enables the reader to instantly make sense of the words on the paper and once you've enjoyed a book, you might usefully go back and read it again to look at sentence structure. The simple grammar. The skeleton that supported the story while you were concentrating on what was happening to the hero and heroine.

For those of you who are a little hazy on the basics, I can heartily recommend *Getting the Point* by Elizabeth Hawksley and Jenny Haddon (former chairwoman of the Romantic Novelists' Association).

It's a light-hearted and simple guide to grammar.

Oh, and "its" means "of it"; "it's" means "it is" or "it has"

EDITING

There is no finer way of polishing your manuscript until it sparkles than by shutting yourself away from all interruptions and reading it aloud. You'll spot repetitions that the familiar eye would slide over. You'll become aware of errors in punctuation — my right ring finger dabs in extraneous commas with a wild abandon that has nothing to do with my brain or my grasp of grammar.

You'll catch any similarity in the "voices" of your character — and not because you're doing all the voices. Every character should "sound" different to the reader. Mature characters use different language to younger ones. Men use different — and fewer — words to women to express the same emotion.

You'll spot the overlong sentence, clumsy phrasing.

Finally, before you submit your manuscript to an agent or

publisher, put it aside for as long as you can bear — at the very least a week — and then re-read it through carefully once more. If you can, ask someone else read it; not to comment on your prose, but to pick up mistakes in spelling, typing and trip-up sentences that you know so well you will not notice them.

SUBMISSION

All manuscripts, whether submitted online or as hard copy should be presented in double spacing in a plain, readable font — Times New Roman is perfect — no smaller than 12 point and with 2.5 cm of white space all around.

Indent your paragraphs — don't leave an extra line between paragraphs except to indicate a scene change. Use a header or footer with your real name, the book title and the page number.

If you are submitting to Harlequin Mills and Boon, use your national standard spelling and grammar; color in the US, colour in the UK, for example and double speech marks " —"in the US, '—' single ones in the UK.

Each publisher will have guidelines for submission on their website. Most will ask for the first three chapters of your manuscript and a synopsis.

The synopsis should be one or two pages, single spaced and be a summary of the whole story, including the ending. It should summarize all major plot points, give a flavour of the book — tender, funny, emotional. It should tell the editor the important things about your hero and heroine and (if it's an historical) the period in which it is set.

You will need a query letter with which you will —

- introduce yourself briefly
- mention any special expertise that is relevant to your book. If it's a medical romance, for instance, it would be appropriate to mention medical training.
- say which series or imprint it is intended for
- list publication credits, but only for work for which you have been paid.

Keep to the point, keep it professional. Use your own name, not a pseudonym and do not mention that your mother/sister/best mate thinks this is the best book she's ever read.

SOME FURTHER READING

12 Points of Writing Romance by Kate Walker
Love Writing by Sue Moorcroft
On Writing Romance by Leigh Michaels
The Fire in Fiction by Donald Maas
Goal, Motivation and Conflict by Debra Dixon
Dangerous Men and Adventurous Women edited by Jayne Ann
Krentz
Write It Forward by Bob Mayer
The Creative Habit by Twyla Tharp
Save the Cat by Blake Snyder
The Romance Fiction of Mills and Boon by jay Dixon
Getting the Point by Elizabeth Hawksley and Jenny Haddon

   and, just for fun —

   Charles Schulz's Snoopy's Guide to the Writing Life edited by
Barnaby Conrad and Monte Schulz with generous writing advice to
Snoopy from authors as distinguished as Ray Bradbury and as
popular as Danielle Steele and Julia Child

   Magazines for writers and readers —

   Writers News UK
   Writer's Forum UK
   Mslexia UK
   Romantic Times BOOKclub magazine US
   Writer's Digest US

SOME WRITING ORGANISATIONS

Romantic Novelists' Association

The RNA was formed in 1960 to promote romantic fiction and to encourage good writing and now represents more than 700 published writers, agents, editors and other publishing professionals

The RNA has a New Writers' Scheme for unpublished writers which includes a full critique of a manuscript by an author published in the same genre. The numbers are limited so get your application in at the beginning of January.

They hold an annual conference, attended by industry professionals, where appointments with agents and publishers are much sought after. There are summer and Christmas parties where New Writers can network with writers and industry professionals. They also hold regular meetings in London with agents, publishers and writers as guest speakers and have regional groups throughout the country.

The RNA Awards Reception is a major event with awards for both mainstream and genre romance fiction.

http://www.rna-uk.org/

Romance Writers of America

For both published and unpublished writers with local chapters and online help. The RITA®, the RWA annual award for the very best in published fiction, is the romance industry equivalent of the Oscar.

The annual RWA Golden Heart© contest for unpublished manuscripts is run alongside the RITA® and local chapters also run competitions for published and unpublished authors.

The RWA national conference is a major event and attended by industry professionals. Agent appointments are much sought after.

http://www.rwa.org

Romance Writers of Australia

Support for published and unpublished writers, with established competitions and an annual conference attended by writers and industry professionals.

www.romanceaustralia.com

Romance Writers of New Zealand

Support for published and unpublished writers, with established competitions and an annual conference attended by writers and industry professionals.

www.romancewriters.co.nz

NINC – Novelists Inc.

An organisation for writers who have published at least two books.

www.ninc.com

SOME ROMANCE PUBLISHERS' WEBSITES

Harlequin — www.harlequin.com

You'll find helpful information at the bottom of the homepage under "write for us"

Harlequin Mills and Boon — www.millsandboon.co.uk

You'll find helpful information at the bottom of the homepage under "write for us"

Samhain Publishing — www.samhainpublishing.com

ChocLit Publishing — www.choclitpublishing.com

Entangled Publishing — www.entangledpublishing.com

Rouge — www.rougeromance.co.uk

Wild Rose Press — http://thewildrosepress.com/

Loveswept – www.romanceatrandom.com/category/loveswept/

Avon Impulse —www.avonromance.com/impulse/

Carina Press — http://carinapress.com/blog/submission-guidelines/

This list is not exhaustive. There are new eBook publishers appearing all the time, but the above are established print and ebook publishers with a track record.

Never pay an agent or publisher to read your book.

Reputable agents and publishers do not ask for money.

ABOUT THE AUTHOR

Liz Fielding is the author of more than sixty romances and has been nominated seven times for the Romance Writers' of America RITA® award, winning twice with *The Best Man & the Bridesmaid* and *The Marriage Miracle*. She has also been nominated three times for the UK's Romantic Novelists' Association "Romance Prize", winning with *A Family of His Own*.

She has also received a Lifetime Achievement Award from Romantic Times BOOKclub magazine

MORE BY LIZ FIELDING

Recent books, available in paper and eBook format,
by Liz Fielding —

The Last Woman He'd Ever Date
Chosen As the Sheikh's Wife
Flirting With Italian
Tempted By Trouble
Mistletoe and the Lost Stiletto
A Wedding at Leopard Tree Lodge
Secret Baby, Surprise Parents
SOS: Convenient Husband Required
and
Secret Wedding — Mollie Blake's story, from which the quotes at
the beginning of each chapter are taken.
The Bride's Baby (free download)

Also available in eBook format —

Wild Justice (free download)
Wild Lady
Wild Fire

You will find a full list of books written by Liz Fielding on her
website — http://www.lizfielding.com

Printed in Great Britain
by Amazon

50480302R00059